Table of Contents

Walking Out of Darkness

Moving Beyond Loss and Living a More Fulfilling Life

By Bridget Anne Carley and Scott David O'Reilly

To Margaret,
Regards,
Bridget

Love [is] between the mortal and the immortal. . . . [It is] a grand spirit which brings together the sensible world and the eternal world and merges them into one great whole."

-- Diotima

"Thousands of candles can be lighted from a single candle, and the life of the candle will not be shortened. Happiness never decreases by being shared."

-- The Buddha

Love is patient and kind . . . Love bears all things, believes in all things, hopes all things, and endures all things.

-- Corinthians

If you want happiness for an hour -- take a nap. If you want happiness for a day -- go fishing. If you want happiness for a month -- get married. If you want happiness for a year -- inherit a fortune. If you want happiness for a lifetime -- help someone else.

-- Chinese Proverb

The most important thing in life is to learn how to give out love, and to let it come in.

-- Morrie Schwartz

This book is dedicated in loving memory to Pat, Jim, Mary and Joseph Sr.

Preface

Humans have memorialized their deceased loved ones since the dawn of mankind. One of the most affecting memorials was created by the artist Käthe Kollwitz for her son, Peter, who was killed in World War I. Her memorial, *Grieving Parents*, consists of two statues: a mother and father, side by side, but alone in their grief. Poignantly, Kollwitz placed her memorial so that it is overlooking not only her son's grave, but also every other grave in the cemetery. In a sense, Kollwitz's statue stands as a testament to the human spirit as it seeks to transform pain and suffering into something that is both beautiful and comforting to others. We cannot undo death or bring our loved ones back, but we can find ways to memorialize their lives in ways that make the world a better and more hopeful place.

Introduction

What is done in love is done well

-- Vincent Van Gogh

Human beings can be like clouds; we are both magnificent and impermanent. The transience of existence is one of the hardest things to accept about life. We treasure the beauty of a flower, a loved one, or an afternoon sky, but we are naturally sad when the beauty that has filled us with awe and a deep appreciation for life's bounties passes beyond our reach. We want to hold on to those we love, but the gifts of life go hand in hand with the reality of death. The greater the beauty, the dearer a loved one is to us, the greater our sense of loss when that someone is taken away from us.

We cannot do away with death, for it is a part of life. We cannot bring our departed loved ones back. But we can find ways to weave their stories, wisdom, and love into the tapestry of our lives. Once we have come to terms with death, then the deep and lasting impressions our loved ones have left upon us can help us to lead healthier, happier, and more fulfilled lives. We carry the memory of our loved ones within us. These memories can glow like a flame that lights our way through the darkness. The beloved that have gone before us would want to us to live and love fully. This book is about finding ways to rekindle the love and light they gave us so that we might have brighter lives.

Feeling the Loss

"We love our dear ones deeply and miss them when they leave us. But we know that the bond of love is greater than death."

-- Harold Klemp

A procession of clouds stretched across the horizon. New clouds continually came into view as others passed beyond my sight. It was shortly after my mother's passing, and I was taking a plane trip. Gazing out the window, I gave some thought to my life. Letting my mind wonder I peered at the radiant sunshine, and the ground below, which at times resembled a patchwork quilt. The clouds were imbued with an effervescent glow as a hazy fog slowly crept across the sky. I was awestruck by nature, the mystery of creation, and how life and death are intertwined. We normally tend to think of life and death as opposites, but death is actually a natural progression in life. From an early age we are taught that death is a part of life, but many times we do not really come to grips with that idea until it directly affects us. Death certainly ends life, but it does not end our relationships with our loved ones. Our memories of them can sustain us through the rest of our lives.

The loss of a loved one can leave us with a gaping hole in our lives. Often, the pain of the moment can seem unbearable and overwhelming. The mourning process is natural. However, we would do a disservice to both ourselves and our loved ones if we allowed the loss we feel to dominate the rest of our lives. I believe our loved ones would want us to experience happiness, find meaning, and make the most of our lives. The loss of a loved one will always be a part of our journey, but loss need not sit in the driver's seat.

We cannot drive looking in the rearview mirror, nor can we live focused on the past. By this I mean we cannot live each day carrying the burdens, anger, and sadness of yesterday. We must try to move forward with each new day. We can, of course, glance in the rearview mirror of life, as we do not want to erase the past. But our focus needs to be on the path ahead. In particular, we need to appreciate the quality of time we have with those family members and friends that still surround us. We do not want to have regrets that we did not spend ample time with them because we were consumed with living in the past. Memories that are so heart wrenching at first, will become deeply appreciated and dearly treasured over time. We must try and seize the moment. After all, that is all any of us are guaranteed. In the memorable words of Alice Morse Earle, "The clock is running. Make the most of today. Time waits for no man. Yesterday is history. Tomorrow is a mystery. Today is a gift. That's why it is called the present."

I find living in the present is a good antidote to stress. Stress is an understandable and unavoidable response to the loss of a loved one. However, it is important not to let stress get the better of us. Stress can be debilitating in that it can affect us in various ways. Stress can affect us physically, emotionally and spiritually. If you can take a moment during a stressful time and reflect on at least one good or beautiful thing in your life, then you can at least partially defuse the stress.

On the other hand, fixating on negative emotions can exacerbate stress during the grieving process. The loss of a loved one frequently aggravates family tensions and resentments. However, by carrying a grudge, anger, or resentment for just one hour actually means you are cheating yourself out of sixty minutes of happiness.

It is so important to find sanctuaries of happiness. Stress builds up in the body and it can take a toll on our physical health and emotional well-being. Even during the darkest periods of grief it is essential to find ways to alleviate the stress we feel. Different people will gravitate towards different activities to help lessen stress. However, I find walking to be an especially therapeutic way of coping with the grieving process. There is so much emphasis today on exercise, but just taking a walk can be a simple, no-cost way of refreshing your body, mind, and spirit.

I find it is very helpful to go for a walk, but walking with an open mind and a positive attitude can be especially therapeutic. Exercise can be healing in itself, but a little exercise while experiencing nature can be even more beneficial. So, instead of just taking a walk, try to take a walk with meaning and purpose. By this, I mean be aware and appreciative of your surroundings. Take the time to look at the green blades of grass that blanket the ground. Savor the multicolored flowers that abound. Glance at the blue sky, the clouds, and the trees with their branches as they sway in the wind. Listen to the laughter of children, the music of birds chirping, and the wind rustling through the foliage. It is not only the walk that is important, but it may be what you see, hear or who you meet along the way that has an impact on you and a healing effect. It is important to pay close attention to everything we do in life, because what we say, hear or do has an effect on our lives.

Whenever you meet someone he or she will naturally form an impression. This impression will be either positive or negative, so why not try your best in life to create a positive impression and bring out the best in others? Being positive and looking for the positive in others can create a virtuous dynamic, which can be especially helpful in our journey through the grieving process.

Some people are like supernovas; they give off light. Other people can be like black holes; they suck the life and energy out of everything they come in contact with. In my view, people who are supernovas have an attitude of love and caring towards the world. Conversely, people who are black holes seem consumed by anger, resentment, and grievances. From my experience, aligning oneself with love gives one the strength and power to overcome adversity and cope with the challenges life throws at us. On the other hand, fear, anger, and negativity tend to sap one's strength.

The death of a loved one can stir up feelings of rage and anger. How could God, a higher power, or life deal us such a horrific blow? Feelings of anger and rage can be inevitable and to some extent natural. However, it would be a double tragedy if we allow negative emotions to dominate our lives and derail our potential to live fully. It is important to find ways to respond to the death of a loved one constructively rather than destructively. In short, we must find ways to turn the pain of our individual loss into compassion for our fellow travelers.

After I lost my mother I joined a local bereavement group at Holy Name Hospital in New Jersey. Here I met with others who had also suffered a grievous loss. We came together to share our stories and support each other. Our circumstances and backgrounds often differed, but we shared a common experience: the death of someone very dear to us. We all felt a deep sense of having been wounded by death, but we had to find ways to help each other heal and continue on in life.

The death of a loved one can stop us in our tracks. It is easy to get stuck in a rut of pain and suffering. Often, it seems like things will never get back to normal. Sometimes, it seems that happiness is gone forever. At times like this it can seem like despair is a cloud that will never lift. However, no matter how great the pain we can still find ways to bring beauty and meaning into our lives by honoring, emulating, and incorporating the spirit of our loved ones in our daily lives.

While attending my bereavement group I met a woman named Barbara who shared a very poignant and inspiring story. Barbara lost her son Robert to a rare blood disease, histiocytosis, when he was just twenty-eight. Barbara's grief was almost unbearable when I first met her. But she managed to transform her personal pain into a sense of purpose by organizing an annual charity walk in her son's memory. In this way, Barbara knows that she is helping other mothers and their children to find better treatments that will hopefully overcome this dread disease in the future.

We cannot alter the fact of death. But we can choose how we respond to it. Barbara found ways to create meaning and purpose in her life that helped her fill the void following her son's death. Instead of succumbing to sadness she decided to do something proactive for others connected to the condition that took her son's life. Her activities will not bring back her son, but it may help save other mothers from experiencing a similar loss. Barbara's mission gives her life a meaning and purpose, which helps her cope with her loss. It does not end her pain, but it helps transform her pain into something constructive, even beautiful.

We are creatures that have a thirst for meaning and purpose. The philosopher Aristotle believed that humans are goal-directed creatures. Just as flowers orient themselves to the sun, humans orient themselves towards a moral horizon. Ideally, we all strive to fulfill our potential, to be the best persons we can be. When we set goals and accomplish them, we create meaning for ourselves. When we find meaning it gives us a sense of inner-satisfaction and happiness. On the other hand, a lack of meaning or purpose can lead to feelings of dissatisfaction and unhappiness.

The loss of a loved one is bound to make us sad. It takes time to come to terms with loss. However, I believe our loved ones would want us to experience the joys and miracles of life. One way we can do this is to honor the memory of our loved ones and to celebrate all the good moments we shared with them. For example, my father passed away some years ago. To me he was a loving dad, the pillar of our family, and a wonderful role model. He exemplified decency, hard work, and a commitment to excellence. In so many ways, he was my beacon and guiding light because I always looked to him when I needed to find my bearings in life.

After my father died we held a small memorial service to honor his life. My former teacher and good friend, a Sister of Charity, Sister Elizabeth, planted a small tree in his name. Today, I can still see the tree from my window. In the spring, I often marvel at the tree's pink flowers glistening in the wind as the sun shines on the plaque that bears his name. At night, the plaque often seems to have a florescent glow as it reflects the moonlight.

I feel the power of the sun's and the moon's rays to be magical. Light gives a sense of warmth and goodness. Light makes all things visible, but like the spirit it remains unseen. After all, we never see light per se, only the things which light illuminates. Light, like the spirit, is all around us, but deeply mysterious.

We held a small but intimate ceremony when we dedicated this tree in my father's memory. We recited prayers, sang songs, spoke and reminisced about the good times and fine qualities that he demonstrated. We shed more than a few tears, exchanged hugs, and even shared a few laughs. Then, we sang one of my father's favorite songs, the Irish ballad *Danny Boy.* We also held a balloon launch. Balloons are a sign of celebration. Most of the balloons were star-shaped, which symbolized how our family and friends thought of my dad; he was a guiding light for so many of us. But my mom's balloon was heart-shaped, which symbolized how my father was the love of her life.

For me, the ascending balloons signified the journey of his spirit to the heavens. We all watched the balloons as they defied gravity, escaped ensnaring tree branches, and soared across the sky until they became tiny vanishing dots. Later, we gathered at a nearby restaurant to celebrate my father's life with stories and remembrances. I will treasure that day, as I do all the memories of my dad that glow within my heart.

My father's tree still stands strong through all types of weather. It represents his spirit and helps me to feel his presence in my daily life. I often marvel at how the seasons change my father's tree, yet the tree endures the coldest frosts and bleakest winter nights. In December, the branches are sparse and barren, but come spring my father's tree bursts forth with renewed life as countless pink flowers blossom under the sun's rays. The warmth of the sun and the sweet fragrance of the flowers invigorate my soul and rekindle my faith in the goodness of life.

My father's tree helps keep him alive for me. I have a special bond with his tree. Watching it year by year has nourished my soul, just as my father's love helped me to flourish as a person. It is a living symbol of his spirit, which helps me feel an invisible but deeply rooted connection with him.

The mythologist Joseph Campbell described ritual as the enactment of myth. We tend to think of myths as stories that are not true. But myths have power because they contain poetic truths. That is, myths may not be literally true, but they exhibit deep psychological and spiritual truths. When we create a ceremony to honor our loved ones we are tapping the power of myth; in a sense, we are turning the prose of life into poetry. Rituals help us channel our emotions and can put us in a new frame of mind. Therefore, rituals can be cathartic, liberating, incredibly meaningful, and even transformative.

The ceremony to honor my father was a beautiful day that I will always remember. The event and the tree planting helped provide closure for my family and me. More importantly, the ritual created a fond memory that is a reminder of my dad's goodness. When I think of the ceremony and the tree I am reminded of the deeply-rooted connection I have with my father. This helps to keep his spirit forever alive and growing within in my heart.

The tree we planted to honor my father's memory stands strong through all types of weather. It represents his spirit and helps me to feel his presence in my daily life.

A Sister's Lesson

"Life is rather a state of embryo, a preparation for life; a man is not completely born till he has passed through death."

-- Benjamin Franklin

There is a very touching scene in John Ford's classic film, *She Wore a Yellow Ribbon*, starring John Wayne. In the picture, a retiring cavalry officer named Nathan Brittles (played by Wayne) visits the gravesite of his departed wife. In the twilight hours, he tends to her grave and talks with her as if she were alive, keeping her abreast of the latest family news and the developments in his life. It's a wonderfully played scene and it illustrates how we the living can make the departed real presences in our lives.

The graveyard scene in *She Wore a Yellow Ribbon* is poignant and memorable for many reasons. The tenderness and devotion displayed by Nathan Brittles towards his late wife is heartwarming. We feel his sincerity and the depth of his involvement in an ongoing relationship with his beloved wife. Death may have been the end of their physical contact, but it was not the end of their psychological and spiritual contact.

There is another classic film, *Enchantment*, starring David Niven and Teresa Wright, which makes a similar point. In the film the narrator observes that there are no final endings, only stories than link the past and the future. Death may end our lives, but in a very real sense it does not end our stories. If we lose someone dear to us, we can still weave their stories, and hence something of their essence and spirit, into our lives.

For example, my older sister Pat passed away very unexpectedly at the tender age of twenty-three. Pat was not just my older sister; she was also one of my dearest friends, a role model, and an all-round great person. Like most young people Pat had so much to look forward to and so much to offer. She had just completed college, was embarking on a new career as a special education teacher, and was planning her marriage. Tragically, our hopes for her and her dreams were brought to a halt when she died suddenly of an undiagnosed ailment three days before her wedding.

Elation in our household immediately turned to heartbreak. We were all looking forward to Pat's wedding day; we never imagined that instead we would end up at her funeral. Pat's passing made me realize that death does not discriminate by age. Nevertheless, Pat was a great influence on so many people's lives, including my own. Her life was far too short, but the love she shared and the lessons she taught have guided me for a lifetime.

There is one lesson my sister taught me, which will always stand out in my mind. Shortly before her death, I was a sixteen-year old sophomore in high school trying out for the tennis team. I was anxious about making the team, but my sister Pat helped put my mind at ease with a gesture I'll always remember. The night before the tryouts Pat gave me a t-shirt with a colorful tennis racquet emblazoned on the front. "I am giving you this for two reasons," she said, "if you do not make the team, just remember that you worked hard and tried your best." Working hard and trying your best is what makes you a winner." The second reason Pat gave me the shirt was in case I made the team. It was her way of saying "congratulations" for the hard work and persistence I had shown in achieving my goal. As it happened, I did make the team and I had the good fortune to be a varsity player for all four years. I wore that t-shirt until it was ragged, but Pat's lesson will never wear out on me. In life, it is important to set goals that challenge us to exceed ourselves. We may not always succeed in achieving our aims. However, setting lofty goals and working hard to achieve them can bring out the best in us. Pat taught me that it's alright to fail so long as we give it our best. The biggest mistake of all is not making an effort to reach our goals and better ourselves in the process.

An author named GK Chesterton once said that "anything worth doing is worth doing poorly." Chesterton wasn't saying that poor performance was acceptable. But he was saying that it's alright to be less than perfect if we are pursuing worthy goals. Even a champion tennis player will have begun their career as an unpolished novice. Persistence, passion, patience, and perspiration are the traits we need to improve ourselves and our game. We will make mistakes along the way to our goals. What counts is learning and correcting the mistakes so that we gradually wean them out. This is the way we become the best we can be.

Life is filled with a never-ending series of challenges. We can face these challenges or shirk them. Ultimately, we have to take responsibility for meeting these challenges and taking control of our destiny. The challenges and goals we have in life often seem daunting, but every journey worth taking begins with a single step. It is the first step that is usually the hardest.

Losing a loved one can engender feelings of stagnation. It is very easy to get into a rut after a loved one has died because we are often left numbed, even emotionally paralyzed. However, inertia, complacency, and apathy can become a vicious cycle; the less motivated we feel the less productive and ambitious we become. When we lack clear goals and achievements, then we often fail to get emotional rewards and social approval, which can boost our spirits and spur us on.

When sadness sets in it is important to do something proactive that gets us out of the doldrums. Setting new goals, volunteering, or simply finding a change of scenery can be the catalysts that get us pointed in a healthier direction. Life is filled with endless opportunities, but it is up to us to find them and pursue them. I believe our departed loved ones would want us to live fully, seize new opportunities, and find true happiness. I know my sister Pat would want me to try hard to achieve new goals and improve myself. Setting worthy goals and working towards them is the path to greater happiness and a more fulfilled life. This is the lesson my big sister Pat gave me and I feel she would be very proud if she knew how much it has meant to me and helped me in my life.

Creating Happiness

"Death is not the greatest loss in life. The greatest loss is what dies inside us while we live."

-- Norman Cousins

I love finding still moments when I can immerse myself in the wonders of nature. I love watching tall trees sway in the wind, delicate birds as they flutter from branch to branch, and the sight of clouds as they drift across a brilliant blue sky. Each day is unique and brings new wonders. Each moment is an act of creation in which I play a part.

I often think of the words of Emily Dickinson when I am contemplating the mysteries of nature: She wrote:

The Brain is wider than the sky,
For, put them side by side,
The one the other will include
With ease, and you beside.

The brain is deeper than the sea,
For, hold them blue to blue,
The one the other will absorb,
As sponges, buckets do.

The brain is just the weight of God,
For, lift them pound for pound,
And they will differ, If they do,
As syllable from sound.

The late Princeton physicist John Wheeler proposed an idea called "genesis by observership." In essence, Wheeler believed that Creation was not just some moment in the distant past, but an ongoing process that we play a part in. In other words, life is open-ended and we have the opportunity to fill in some of the blanks.

You might say we are all potential artists. Our emotions, attitudes, and outlooks are part of the palette we draw upon as we add our brushstrokes to the canvas of life.

A philosopher named Ludwig Wittgenstein believed that "a depressed person lives in a depressed world." I find this to be an important insight. A person who approaches life with a negative outlook and who always sees the glass as half empty is going to inhabit a gloomy world. Emotions, at least to some extent, are a choice. Most of us are bound to face painful and sad circumstances in life, but we can also choose to focus our attention on family, friends, beauty, and the other good things that surround us.

George Bernard Shaw once said, "Life does not cease to be funny when people die any more than it ceases to be serious when people laugh." When we experience the death of a loved one, then a very natural reaction is that life comes to a sudden halt. There are feelings of sadness and grief that follow, and many other emotions. We can feel very alone, but outside of our circle there is still laughter and joy in the world. In due time, I believe our departed loved ones would want us to find and experience that happiness.

Death is very difficult to come to grips with, especially when it hits close to home. It is hard to accept that death is a part of life and that death occurs all the time. The sting of death can leave us feeling numb and emotionally paralyzed. Yet it is important to realize that life will and should go on. Often, it is helpful to take the focus off what we've lost following a death and instead try to appreciate all we've gained from our loved one during their lifetime. As we begin to heal, it is important to remember that laughter and happiness still exist and that one day they will return to us.

The poet Robert Frost said: "In three words I can sum up everything I've learned about life: *it goes on.*" This is a simple, but profound idea. The older I become the more meaningful Frost's insight has become. I've had many wonderful experiences, but also many tragic and sad events too. But in each case life goes on. Some things in life we can control, but some we cannot, but in either case ... life goes on.

Experience has taught me that it is up to each of us to make the most of every moment. We all need time to grieve, but it is also important not to let loss dominate our attention and consume us. I like to think of each moment with a loved one as a gift and a blessing. We only have a brief time on this earth, but that makes each moment we are allotted all the more precious. We can try and fill our moments with love. For me, moments filled with love always seem to glow in the memory. On the other hand, time dominated by negative and dysfunctional emotions seem to me to be moments that are squandered. I like to think of love as a brightly colored thread that stitches together the best moments in the tapestry of our lives. It is up to us to create a pattern we can look back upon with fondness.

A Father's Wisdom

"We are what we repeatedly do. Excellence is not an act but a habit."

-- Aristotle

"Pleasure in the job puts perfection in the work"

-- Aristotle

My father taught me a very important lesson: "Do the right thing," he once said, "and you can never be wrong." Sometimes the truth hurts and the results may not always be advantageous, but as long as you did the right thing you can be at peace with yourself and your decision. My dad didn't just teach me this lesson, he exemplified it.

My dad was a firm believer in teaching us the right way to do things and he discouraged us from cutting any corners. When it came to the simplest chores, such as raking the leaves, shoveling the snow, or carrying groceries, he encouraged excellence. As a child, of course, I just wanted to get the job done as quickly as possible.   For example, while carrying groceries in from the car I often tried to manage as many bags as possible in one trip, which usually resulted in my dropping some of the items.

Cutting corners seemed like a shortcut, but in long run it took me longer and I was less productive. I can recall many instances when my father would say, "Do not carry a lazy man's load." Today, I can appreciate how his advice can apply to so many situations. I've learned that doing things thoroughly and with an eye towards excellence allows me to do what I'm doing more precisely and efficiently. Invariably, this helps me get the job done right. This is just a very simple example, but my father's philosophy in life was to always strive for excellence in whatever you do, no matter how large or small the task.

Everything my father did he tried to do with care. If he was hanging a picture he would take careful measurements and approach each step methodically with the upmost care. He was an engineer and he realized that precise planning was the key to making things work properly. I didn't realize it at the time, but years later I came to appreciate that my father's way of doing things resembled the habits of mind that the philosopher Aristotle associated with the man of virtue and excellence.

Aristotle was a great believer in habits. To be a good athlete, musician, or craftsman meant repeating specific actions again and again until they became second nature. The same can be said of morality; we become virtuous by performing moral actions repeatedly. For instance, an ax that is sharp just *some* of time isn't going to fulfill its function. Good habits keep us sharp and pointed in the right direction. Good habits help make us the best individuals we can be.

My father was a genuinely cheerful person. I believe his happiness derived from his commitment to excellence and his personal and professional success. He set ambitious goals for himself. When he accomplished them he felt satisfied. In a sense, we can think of happiness as the point of a compass directing us towards excellence. This Aristotelian outlook implies that all of nature is inherently goal directed. For example, the acorn strives to be an oak tree; the caterpillar's aim is to become a butterfly; the individual seeks to realize his or her full potential. When we achieve our aims we are happy. Conversely, when we are thwarted from our goals we are dissatisfied. I believe that we should choose aims and goals that are worthy of our humanity, bring out our best, and express our deepest aspirations.

Aristotle tied happiness to excellence and ethics. We are happiest when we are exercising our own special excellence and fulfilling our highest potential. My dad took great pride in doing everything to the best of his ability. He knew that planning ahead and doing things in a meticulous way invariably yielded the best results. He never lost sight of his goal, but he also did things in a step by step manner. Aristotle believed that virtue and excellence were the keys to a fulfilled and productive life. I believe my dad was living proof of that wisdom.

Aristotle believed the virtuous man hewed to something called the Golden Mean. The Golden Mean is the middle ground between two extremes. Prudence is the middle ground between the extremes of stinginess and extravagance. Courage is the middle ground between cowardice and recklessness. Wisdom is the middle ground between ignorance and mere cunning. Avoiding extremes and sticking to a middle path, according to Aristotle, was the surest route towards a happy and fulfilled life.

The ancient Greeks believed that beauty was composed of three elements: symmetry, proportion, and harmony. I believe my dad possessed these three characteristics. He led a balanced life. He enjoyed life's pleasures, but he was never indulgent. He was a man of reason, but he was also kind, attentive, and emotionally warm. Whenever he felt the need to discipline my siblings and me he would always explain his reasoning in a gentle but firm manner. In all my years, I never heard him utter an unkind or angry word towards my mother. I respect the traits he exhibited, but even more I love the man who embodied and lived by them.

I am often quite touched by how much admiration my dad inspired. Recently, I heard my brother-in-law describe my father as the "finest man I've ever known." I was deeply moved by the conviction in his voice. My father's keen intellect, his integrity, and his rock-solid character made a deep impression on all who knew him. Of course, I also looked up to my father for many other reasons; his personal warmth, his sense of humor, and his fun-loving attitude. I have such vivid memories of my younger brother Jim and me marching behind my dad like little ducklings every Sunday following church as we made our way to a local bakery for treats. In so many respects, my dad always put us on the right path. Furthermore, my father's example and the love he shared has guided my remaining siblings and me throughout our lives.

There was a harmony in my dad's soul. Plato believed that every individual consists of a "reasoning" part, an "emotional" part, and an "appetitive" part. The well-rounded and harmonious person strikes a balance between these three aspects of our psychological makeup. Most of us would probably agree that reason should govern, so as to keep the emotions and appetites in check, but each element is an essential part of who we are. My dad seemed to exhibit that harmony better than anyone I've ever known.

I always put my father on a pedestal as he was a dedicated husband, wonderful father, terrific grandfather, and an inspiration to his employees and everyone he came in contact with in his life. Though he lived a full life, in his later years he was diagnosed with cancer. Learning my father had a dread disease that would take his life was one of the saddest moments in my life. His initial prognosis was three to four years, but we were most fortunate in that he lived on this earth with us for ten years. My dad was most insistent that no one outside our family was to be told about the seriousness of his illness. He was not embarrassed by his condition; he simply did not want to be treated any differently because he had a terminal illness. I loved my father dearly and was devastated by his loss, but I also deeply admired the composure my father displayed as he faced his mortality.

My father displayed a stoic attitude towards his illness. My father had a great love for life, but he also had a clear-headed understanding of his fate. I believe he maintained his emotional composure not only for himself, but also to shield our family from as much anguish as possible.

My father's brave face was a comfort to our family, but I can also appreciate how others may benefit from talking about, expressing, and sharing emotions regarding their illness. When confronted with a terminal condition, each of us must choose the path that we feel is best for us and our families.

The term stoicism is associated with emotional composure and an acceptance of one's fate. There is a perennial debate between accepting the cards life deals us and refusing to bow to fate. Sometimes, we may try to resist death with all our might. Other times, accepting the inevitable may lead to peace of mind. Each individual and circumstance is unique.

Should we accept our fate or chart our own destiny? Perhaps the dilemma each of us faces is best captured by the well-known Serenity Prayer by the theologian

Reinhold Neibuhr: "Lord grant me the serenity to accept the things I cannot change, the courage to change the things I can, and the wisdom to know the difference."

I loved my father dearly and I have great admiration for the courageous attitude he took towards his own illness and mortality. My father's equanimity in the face of death was a comfort to my family and me. We took some solace in the fact that he had made the most of every day and lived a full life.

My father was a man of emotional depth, but I'm sure he had teary moments, which he kept to himself. Stoic resolve is to be respected, but emotional composure must be balanced against an emotional openness to love. To love and be loved means being vulnerable. Receiving true and unconditional love from another person is one of the most validating and nourishing gifts we can experience. Emotional composure is a good thing, so long as we remain open to others and the gift of love.

My father possessed a keen intellect and was a man with a wide range of interests. He was curious about life and enjoyed speculating about scientific matters, moral questions, and the mysteries of life, but he was also very down-to-earth and well-rounded. As a result, he had a remarkable knack for conversing and getting along with people from all walks of life. Whether talking with an engineer or an auto-mechanic, my dad always seemed bring out the best in people.

My father could be very disciplined and meticulous. Today, as my siblings and I reminisce about our childhood, we often marvel at how he could run a business, manage a household, and have so much time for our family. Our father set very high standards, which he demanded of himself and encouraged in us, but he always explained why he set the bar so high.

When you are young, rules and discussions of right and wrong can seem like impediments to freedom. Today, however, as I reflect on my childhood, I can see why my dad wanted to teach us the right way of doing things. Morality, discipline, and high standards are important because they help individuals, families, and societies thrive.

My dad had a code he lived by, but those high standards meant so much to him because family meant so much to him. This lesson was brought home to me as I think about my father's last days. He had always been a bear of a man, sturdy and strong, so it was especially difficult and poignant to know we were caring for him instead of him caring for us, as he always had. He gathered our family around him so he could tell us: "stay together," "look out for one another," and "family matters."

Those two words – "family matters" – sum up everything my father lived for and aimed at. He set high standards, but he always explained them and his reasoning to us. Just as importantly, he was a great listener. He valued our perspective and encouraged us to think for ourselves. But the perennial theme I discern in all he taught us is this: care for each other.

My father would be very proud that we are such a close knit family. Today, three generations of Carleys still gather regularly to celebrate and carry on our family's traditions. There is a plaque in my niece's home that sums up my father's wisdom – "Family Matters." Today, I can appreciate that it is my father's wisdom that is essential to our family's flourishing.

Chasing Rainbows

Carpe Diem (Seize the Day)

-- Quintus Horatius Flaccus

"It's being here now that's important. There's no past and there's no future. Time is a very misleading thing. All there is ever, is the now. We can gain experience from the past, but we can't relive it; and we can hope for the future, but we don't know if there is one."

-- George Harrison

Ireland is a land suffused with timeless beauty. In 1996, I arrived with my younger brother Jim for a short but memorable visit. Upon arriving we saw boundless fields of green, majestic mountains, and the mist as it crept across the landscape.

No postcard, book, or description can capture the hospitality and enchantment one can find in Ireland. I often felt like we were chasing rainbows as we made our way throughout the countryside, with a special treasure awaiting us just on the far side of the horizon.

One day, while staying at a grand Irish hotel, Jim and I learned that we had just narrowly missed the chance of enjoying one of Ireland's national treasures. Apparently, the singer Van Morrison had been staying at the hotel and performing nearby and we had just missed the opportunity of seeing him in concert. Jim and I were both disappointed that we had just narrowly missed one of our favorite singers. But Jim, in his characteristic easygoing and upbeat manner, simply insisted that we'd be sure to see Van Morrison on our next visit.

My brother Jim passed away unexpectedly just months after our venture to Ireland. He had been out on a routine jog, an activity he loved, when he suffered a heart attack. He was just thirty-five and the picture of health and vitality, but we learned later that he had an undiagnosed heart ailment, which proved to be a silent killer. Losing Jim was one of the most painful experiences in my life. But I will be forever grateful for every moment we were able to enjoy together.

I'm so thankful I have the wonderful memories of the trip Jim and I took to Ireland. In fact, our trip almost didn't happen. My father was battling cancer at the time. Initially, we hoped both he and my mom would join us for a family vacation, but at the last minute my father's doctors insisted he was not well enough to make the trip. I expected we would cancel our plans altogether, but my father was insistent that Jim and I go as planned. "Life is for the living" he said, "go and make the most of everyday."

The memories of my trip to Ireland with Jim are so vivid that it is hard to believe it has been sixteen years since he passed away. I believe that the right kind of experiences and opportunities can enhance our memories; and memories and recollections can help sustain the spirit of our loved ones long after they have passed.   For example, in 2013, by complete coincidence my boyfriend happened to notice that Van Morrison was performing at a historic setting in Ireland. He asked me if I'd like to plan a venture together. The idea of hearing Van Morrison in Ireland captivated both of us. I was so struck by the connection to Jim that I immediately felt it was an opportunity that we had to seize. With this in mind, I made the decision to return to Ireland to hear Van Morrison sing at Dunluce Castle, a 13th century ruin perched on a cliff overlooking the North Sea.

We arrived in Ireland on June 7th, the date of Jim's birthday. As chance had it, the weather that week was some of the fairest the country had seen in more than half a decade. Clear blue skies, green fields and sunshine greeted us as we made our way to County Antrim, situated on the North Sea, home of Dunluce Castle and many other natural and man-made attractions.

The next morning we hiked about four miles from a local bed & breakfast to the historic remnants of Dunluce Castle. We had arrived early, and portions of the castle were still enveloped in a mist of clouds, which seemed to crawl upwards along the cliffs from the sea. As we peered out towards the North Sea from the remnants of a castle window we spied a rainbow, which formed an arc beginning in the sands, stretching towards the sky, before ending in the ocean. Before our trip, my boyfriend and I had talked about chasing rainbows in Ireland in a figurative sense. But here a real rainbow had come out to greet us on the first full day of our venture. We both had an unmistakable sense that my late brother Jim was right there with us in spirit as we marveled at the multi-colored apparition that hovered before us.

Later that day, we hiked to the town of Bushmills, home of the world famous Bushmills Distillery, where we shared an afternoon toast. Then, it was off to Carrikarede, a small island off the coast that is linked to the mainland by a narrow rope bridge. Words can't even begin to describe the beauty of this Irish coastline. The sea water was a translucent aqua green that was so fresh and clear that you could see the pattern of the sands and rocks beneath the waves several feet below. Jagged rock cliffs were dotted with patches of green grass and flowers bloomed in unexpected places. Wherever one turned, the landscape seemed drenched with beauty and teeming with life.

There are days when the mystery and miracle of life seem especially palpable. Days when the beauty we encounter is so overwhelming that it seems that God must be an artist and the world his palette; when we are surrounded by such beauty, the soul blossoms.

Seventeen years earlier my brother Jim and I had missed seeing Van Morrison sing by a day. At the time, it never occurred to me that there would be no "next time" for Jim. Sometimes life is like that; opportunities are fleeting and they may not come again. It is up to us to seize the moment and live as fully as possible. That evening, on the same day that my boyfriend and I miraculously encountered a rainbow at Dunluce Castle, and crossed the Carrick-a-Rede rope bridge, Van Morrison sang for us at the edge of the North Sea under an Irish sky. There were many thousands of other souls there too, dancing, singing along, and swaying in the cool evening breeze as Van's soulful voice wafted through the air. Jim was there too, in my heart, smiling as I smiled because I was fulfilling his dream for him.

We visited many fascinating sites during our stay in Ireland. One of our most memorable stops was at the historic Kilmainham Gaol (Jail) in Dublin. On the tour of the jail, which is now a museum, we learned of the moving story of Joseph Plunkett and Grace Gifford. Joseph was a political prisoner sentenced to death for his part in the so-called Easter Rising, an ill-fated Irish independence movement. The night before his execution Plunkett, just twenty-eight, was allowed to marry his fiancée, Grace Gifford, in the prison chapel. After their ceremony, they were given ten-minutes alone. Plunkett was executed just hours later. One can only imagine how the two must have felt; how the prospect of imminent mortality must have heightened the love they had for one another.

On the final full day of our trip to Ireland my boyfriend and I visited St. Michan's Church in Dublin, site of a historic graveyard and crypts which house mummified remains dating back at least four centuries. According to legend, Dublin native Bram Stoker visited the crypts before writing his famous novel, *Dracula*. Undoubtedly, the crypts, which exist underneath the church itself, are more than a little eerie. It's a sobering experience to descend the stone stairways into the underground vaults, which contain remains that reportedly date back to the Crusades.

The mummies are an especially uncanny sight, their blackened corpses seeming more ghoulish than human. A shudder of recognition crept through my veins; it is the destiny of all living things to perish. Before ascending into the world of the living, my boyfriend and I embraced. Our visit to Ireland had begun with a rainbow at Dunluce Castle, but now we were kissing in a crypt. The way our venture in Ireland was bookended seemed to me like a metaphor for the human journey. After all, our brief sojourn on earth is like a rainbow: beautiful, ephemeral, and seemingly conjured out of nothing more substantial than a mixture of sunlight and water vapor. Rainbows may be transient, but they are glorious precisely because they reflect the eternal light of the sun.

The ruins of Dunluce Castle, perched on the coast of Northern Ireland, are a timeless reminder of the impermanence of life.

A Mother's Love

Yesterday is gone. Tomorrow has not yet come. We have only today. Let us begin."

-- Mother Teresa

"Life is not about waiting for the storm to pass. It is about learning to dance in the rain."

-- Vivian Green

Perseverance, dedication and determination are three simple, but very powerful words. They are ideals my mom seemed to exemplify and live by.

My mother had a great faith in the goodness of life. Like my father, she had a zest for living and a contagiously positive attitude. I believe my own optimistic outlook on life owes much to her example.

My mother had a wonderful outlook on life. She enjoyed meeting people, socializing, and sharing stories and laughter with friends and family. Even the loss of two of her children could not permanently dampen her spirit. However, there is no doubt that the pain of losing two children was a significant cross to bear that tested her faith in the goodness of life.

Losing two children at a relatively young age was a horrendous blow for my mother. I know she felt both losses keenly and deeply. Yet, my mom always conveyed an inner-strength and warmth, which reassured me and my remaining siblings.

The severity of my mom's loss was brought home to me in an image she once used to describe how the death of her children impacted her. "Losing two children," she said, "is like losing two fingers on one's hand. You are always reminded of what you have lost, and although you are grateful for the three remaining fingers, your hand will never be whole again." Our family unit had been decimated, and two of my mom's five children had died, but my mother knew she still had three remaining children to love and care for. At all times, she was committed to keeping our family functioning, as best as possible.

The image my mom used to describe her loss was haunting, but it also exhibited her determination to carry on for the good of our family. Our family had suffered a grievous blow – and no one had to bear this loss more than my mother – but she was determined to stand strong so the rest of our family could thrive. We cannot undo or change the fact of death. But we can find ways to enjoy and appreciate the moments we are given.

In retrospect, I'm certain my mom had days and moments of sadness, which she kept from us. However, by keeping a brave face she encouraged the rest of our family to move on with life. I loved my mother and I deeply empathize with the heartbreak she undoubtedly suffered. But I admire her perseverance in the face of suffering and adversity. Sometimes, the pains and troubles of the world can seem overwhelming. Nevertheless, I learned from my mom that bearing sorrows is worth it because better days lie ahead. As time passed, it brought me great happiness to see my mom enjoy smiles, laughter, and special moments with the rest of our family, especially her grandchildren and great-grandchildren. She would beam like the sun when she could gather the clan. I remember with especial fondness our annual St. Patrick's Day celebrations at Brady's Fox Hunt Inn, a stateside establishment, which made our family feel like we had stepped back into the land of our fathers and mothers.

I believe my mom was able to persevere through dark times because of her dedication to her family. In short, she was dedicated to something that transcended herself and this commitment gave her the strength to surmount the heartbreak that visited her. She was absolutely determined to see us through the multiple tragedies that befell our family. Without her strength and resolve, I doubt we would have come through things as well as we did.

My mother's positive outlook and attitude has taught me a great deal. In particular, it has helped me in my own quest to try and live life to the fullest and to appreciate each day. We cannot escape death, but we can certainly choose to live life. As the physician Edward J. Stieglitz once said, "The important thing is not how many years in your life but how much life in your years."

My mother lived to the ripe age of eighty-nine, but she always remained young at heart. One time, when my mom was well into her eighties, she went to visit some friends living in a nursing home. I remember her saying, "I'm glad I do not have to be in a place like this with all these old people." In fact, my mom was quite a bit older than many of the residents she was visiting. But the story illustrates how my mom's positive outlook on life kept her young at heart.

Perseverance, dedication, and determination; those three words sum up the ideals my mom exemplified and lived by. Despite heartbreaking losses, my mom never gave up or gave in. She never wavered in her dedication to her family or her determination to persevere until better days arrived. Today, it fills my heart with pride when I hear my nieces, nephews, and other family members tell stories about how my mom's warmth and kindness touched their lives. She had indeed walked through the darkness, but she had also come out on the other side. In doing so she had learned one of life's most important lessons: Everyone will face hardship and adversity in life. Therefore, it is important to show kindness to our fellow travelers.

Losing my mother was a dark period in my life. But over time, as I reflect on the love she exemplified, I can feel my heart glow with the warmth and goodness she shared.

Today, as I write these words, I am thinking of the famous lines from *The Wizard of Oz*. "There is no place like home." Indeed, no matter how far we travel, or where we go, or what we experience, when you have a loving family there is no place like home.

Inspiring Stories

"It is interesting to notice how some minds seem almost to create themselves, springing up under every disadvantage, and working their solitary but irresistible way through a thousand obstacles."

-- Washington Irving

Etymologically

~~Entomolog~~ically speaking, the word "inspire" means "to breathe in spirit." Inspiring people do seem to be in touch with something divine or transcendent. The spiritual spark they exhibit is something they communicate with both their being and their actions. They are not necessarily famous or world historical figures, but they seem to motivate and encourage all those whose lives they touch.

One of the most inspiring people in my life was a woman named Mary Grace. She was the mother of my childhood friends, Eileen and Karen, who I met at the Jersey Shore almost a half-century ago. In 1970, when Mary Grace was still in her early forties, she was diagnosed with breast cancer. She was the mother of six young children, so I'm sure her illness must have caused her incredible personal anxiety. However, if she had any concerns for her own well-being she never showed it. Indeed, I will always remember how upbeat, kind, and concerned she was about others. She may have been facing a deadly illness, but to everyone who knew her she came across as an active, vibrant, and strong woman.

In 1977, Mary Grace was handed an even graver diagnosis. Her physicians told her she had pancreatic cancer and it looked as if she had just months, if not weeks to live. Mary Grace managed to amaze her doctors with her grit and her will to live. Though her illness took its toll on her body; it seemed that her cancer remained in a state of remission for several years. I believe her faith, her determination to be there for her family, and her love of life helped make her stronger than her disease.

In 1981, Mary Grace had a second cancerous breast removed. Her body was ravaged, but her spirit continued to burn brightly. Despite a grim prognosis a decade earlier, and subsequent health hurdles, year after year Mary Grace remained a fixture of our summers on the Jersey Shore. In 1987, Mary Grace's doctors discovered a cancerous spread on her liver. She described her life as like "sitting on a time bomb." Yet Mary Grace's brush with mortality seemed to make her embrace life even more fervently.

Mary Grace passed away in 1990 at the age of sixty-three. She had defied the deadliest cancers for decades. But more than that, she had lived and loved to the fullest in the knowledge that each day she enjoyed could be her last. There is a lesson in Mary Grace's life for all of us.

To those of us who knew her, Mary Grace's life was a miracle. Disease did not conquer Mary Grace; it only seemed to make her more determined. As her body succumbed to illness her spirit seemed only to grow stronger. Perhaps the words of Henry Ford explain Mary Grace's miracle as well as anything. Ford wrote: "Life is a series of experiences, each one of which makes us bigger, even though sometimes it is hard to realize this. For the world was built to develop character, and we must learn that the setbacks and griefs which we endure help us in our marching onward."

Disease can ravage the body, but illness alone cannot destroy the human spirit. Similarly, time and nature can erode the physical, but they cannot diminish our will to persevere. The story of Gert and Andy, two of my mother's life-long friends, illustrates that even the strongest forces nature can unleash are no match for persons with indomitable spirits. Gert and Andy are a couple in their nineties who have lived in Breezy Point, New York, for more than half a century. However, on October 29, 2012, Hurricane Sandy swept furiously through a large area of the North East, including Breezy Point in Queens, New York. Dozens of homes were destroyed and many families were displaced.

Gert and Andy were residents of Breezy Point for well over fifty years, but Hurricane Sandy decimated their home in a matter of hours. The storm had taken virtually everything they had, except their courage, character, and optimistic attitude. Following the storm, most of their neighborhood had been razed to the ground and their community now resembled a war zone. However, friends and nearby residents demonstrated their generosity and compassion by welcoming Gert and Andy into their homes as the two seniors set about rebuilding their lives.

During this time, Gert and Andy counseled less hopeful residents, encouraging them with their words, their personal kindness, and their example. Gert and Andy were guided by a simple but powerful thought: that one day the sun will come out and shine again on the sea community of Breezy Point. They knew it would take time and effort before that day would come, but they were determined to do everything they could to help make that day happen. In 2013, seven months after Hurricane Sandy hit, Gert and Andy returned to the home they rebuilt in Breezy Point.

Though my mom passed away shortly before Hurricane Sandy, I know she would be so proud (but not surprised) by the resilience and character Gert and Andy displayed in the face of adversity. Gert and my mom were friends for more than eighty years. In fact, Gert, my mom, and two sisters named Peggy and Helen, were so close for so long that they were known as the Brooklyn Gals. Over the course of five decades they shared many ups and downs together. However, an adage from Helen, "We'll go on from here," seemed to sum up the can-do and never-give-in spirit the Brooklyn Gals lived by. Hurricane Sandy undoubtedly did great damage, but it couldn't overturn or upend the spirit of two plucky New Yorkers in their nineties who exemplified the motto, "We'll go on from here."

The Brooklyn Gals: Friends for more than eighty years. Their friendship only deepened over the years.

In 1973, baseball's New York Mets were dead last in their division with just a month left to go in the season. A veteran relief pitcher, named Tug McGraw, tried to encourage his teammates by exclaiming "Ya gotta believe!" during a locker room pep talk. As it happened, the phrase caught on and the Mets caught fire the final month by winning 20 of their last 28 games to win the National League East title. The Mets were defeated in the World Series that year by the Oakland Athletics, but McGraw's exclamation has become a rallying cry for the Mets and their fans over the years. In 1986, the Mets pulled off the kind of World Series magic that seemed to exemplify McGraw's slogan. The 1986 Mets, powered by stars like Keith Hernandez, Daryl Strawberry, and Gary Carter, had won their division handily. They had also produced some thrilling come-from-behind wins in the post season against the Huston Astros to make it to the World Series. However, in game six against the Boston Red Sox the Mets found themselves in a virtually impossible situation.

The Mets were down by two runs and had nobody on base. The Red Sox needed just one more out to clinch their first championship since 1918. Improbably, Gary Carter, Kevin Mitchell, and Ray Knight managed to hit consecutive singles. But the Mets were still trailing when the free swinging Mookie Wilson came to the plate. Boston reliever Bob Stanley soon got Mookie down to his last strike, but the plucky Wilson managed to foul off several pitches during his tenacious at bat. Wilson also managed to avoid getting hit by a wild pitch, a feat which allowed the tying run to score. Finally, on the tenth pitch of the at bat, Mookie hit a soft grounder that took an unexpected bound at the last second as it went right through the legs of the first baseman, Bill Buckner. Ray Knight scored the winning run and the Mets went on to win the World Series in game seven.

The Mets had been down to their final strike not once, but several times. Their comeback win is widely regarded as one of the most inspiring and thrilling come-from-behind victories in World Series history. The 1986 Mets never gave in or gave up. Put simply, the embodied Winston Churchill's famous admonition: "Never, never, never give up." Like Churchill, the 1986 Mets were at their best when things looked their bleakest. As a result, the Mets' game six heroics has become part of baseball's folklore.

Sadly, Mets catcher Gary Carter, who had ignited the improbable rally with his two out single, passed away from a brain tumor in 2012. Ironically, Mets reliever Tug McGraw, who coined the phrase "Ya gotta believe!" had also passed away from a similar ailment in 2004. However, the spirit of both men continues to burn brightly. The Tug McGraw Foundation, for instance, is dedicated to helping individuals and families coping with brain tumors. And the Gary Carter Foundation is involved in helping children and families affected by autism. Both Tug McGraw and Gary Carter exemplified a "Ya gotta believe!" attitude. It's an attitude that says: Yes, life may throw you a lot of curveballs, but if you keep your eye on the ball there is always the possibility of hitting a home run!

George Bailey is the name of a fictional character played by Jimmy Stewart in Frank Capra's timeless classic, *It's a Wonderful Life*. However, my boyfriend, Scott, knew a real life George Bailey who was just as inspiring and wonderful as the character Stewart brought to life on the silver screen.

George Bailey was an African-American janitor at an all-white middle school. Mr. Bailey had a quite demeanor, but he always seemed to have a happy disposition and a ready smile. Occasionally, if Scott wasn't exactly keen on finishing his lunch, he would offer Mr. Bailey half a sandwich or a piece of fruit, which Mr. Bailey gratefully accepted.

Many years later, Scott learned that George Bailey had passed away of a heart attack in middle age. Reading Mr. Bailey's obituary, Scott realized that the seemingly modest man he knew as a janitor was really an exceptional individual. George had raised two daughters by himself following the death of his wife. Moreover, he had managed to put both his daughters through medical school on a janitor's salary.

As Scott recalls, "when I think of the lessons I learned in my teenage years, it is the example of George Bailey, which seems to glow so very brightly in my memory. At the time, I never imagined the loss, the burdens, and the responsibilities George Bailey carried on his shoulders. Only later would I appreciate the dignity, steadfastness, and character this humble man undoubtedly possessed. George always seemed to have a smile for me when I met him in the hall or the cafeteria. His sunny manner always seemed to brighten my day. I didn't know Mr. Bailey all that well, but there is no doubt that George Bailey's attitude has left a tremendous impression on me."

There is a very simple but powerful exercise that you can do that will help you have a tremendous impact on people . . . smile! You will not only be helping yourself, but you may just put a smile on someone else's face too.

I think we all know someone in our life that we admire, because in some way they have had to overcome great adversity. A person that comes to my mind is my cousin, Libby. Before her stroke, Libby was an exceptionally energetic woman in her fifties. Devoted to her work, Libby possessed a vivacious and caring personality. Libby and I often met in New York City for dinner and we always shared many laughs. On October of 2012, I received a startling phone call informing me that Libby had suffered a serious stroke. I immediately headed to New York

Medical Center to find Libby lying on her back, staring vacantly at the ceiling. I was in a state of disbelief; just the week prior Libby and I met for dinner and she was upbeat, full of life, and a seeming model of health. At first, things seemed fairly bleak for Libby. However, thanks to excellent medical care and an innate zest for life, Libby has managed to make improvements virtually every day since her stroke.

It is now one year later and Libby has made remarkable progress. Indeed, most who meet her for the first time would never imagine that Libby had survived a life-threatening stroke. It will likely be some time before Libby returns to work, but the essence of her personality – the thoughtful, caring, and attentive person we all loved – is perfectly intact. Libby still faces a very daunting road back, but she has demonstrated that small, incremental improvements on a daily basis can lead to substantial progress over the long term.

Looking back, I believe Libby's indomitably positive attitude was the key to her recovery. Libby did not allow the long and daunting road to recovery to discourage her. Instead, she focused on the here and now and the small steps she could take on a daily basis that would lead to her goal of getting back to normal. Rather than succumb to fear, anxiety, and depression, Libby displayed courage, optimism, and resolve at each and every step on her long journey back. As a result, Libby has proven more than a match for the stroke that nearly felled her. But that doesn't surprise me. After all, Libby's indomitable attitude can be summed up by a quip she frequently uses during her recovery process: "change is inevitable, struggle is an option."

The word "Renaissance" signifies rebirth and renewal. The term, of course, most commonly refers to the period of cultural flowering that took place after the so-called Dark Ages. As it happens, Renaissance is also the name taken by a 1970's era rock group led by vocalist Annie Haslam.

It's been decades since Renaissance's commercial heyday, but on a whim my boyfriend and I decided to see Renaissance in concert when we spied an advertisement for them in a music flyer. We were glad we did. Annie Haslam's amazing operatic voice can still soar like an exotic bird and the classical-style arrangements of many of their songs sounded fresh, inventive, and impressive.

Equally remarkable, Annie had a fractured spine and was singing in a back brace, which she jokingly referred to during the concert as her "night gown." Musical fashions had long since rendered groups like Renaissance commercially passé, but here was a band that was overcoming health setbacks, financial hardships, and other obstacles, but were still creating excellent new music and putting on a tremendous show.

Renaissance's guitarist, Michael Dunford, also made quite an impression that evening. Grey haired and bespectacled, Dunford wielded only an acoustic guitar, not the customary electric one normally associates with rock musicians. Indeed, Michael's stately demeanor and tasteful fretwork conjured up notions of a grandfatherly professor who just happened to be in a rock band because he also happened to be a musical wizard.

Exhilaration was in the air that evening. Annie's voice was in fine fettle, the band was magnificent, and there was talk of an album of new material by next year, their first in more than a decade. Tragically, just a few weeks after such a memorable musical evening we learned that Michael Dunford had passed away suddenly and unexpectedly of a brain aneurysm. He left behind a wife and two young children. The future of Renaissance seemed very much in doubt. Nevertheless, work on the anticipated new album was largely complete. Michael had written most of the new compositions and recorded his guitar parts. It seemed only fitting that the remaining members of Renaissance would do everything they could to see to it that Michael's musical vision became a reality.

Months later, Renaissance released *Grandine il Vento* (which translates to "hail to the wind") to rave reviews. The album was well-named, as it is a fitting testament to the melodic and musical genius of Michael, who was the animating spirit behind so much of the group's music. My boyfriend and I saw Renaissance again just after the new album came out. Choking back tears, Annie related how she had found a feather backstage, which she took as a sign that Michael was in the concert hall that evening. In a way he was; for there were passages of the new music that were as beautiful as the sight of a feather dancing on the breath of God.

Loss, Prayer, and Faith

"The function of prayer is not to influence God, but rather to change the nature of the one who prays."

-- Soren Kierkegaard

Prayer has been likened to a longing of the soul, a bridge to the divine, and a key that unlocks our hearts to God. When I pray, I believe I am sharing my inner-most thoughts and feelings with our Creator. I take it as a matter of faith that my inner-dialogue is really a two-way conversation; that my sincerest and heartfelt thoughts are heard.

Of course, losing a loved one can test our faith, both in God and in life. Sometimes, during dark moments, we may wonder if our sincerest prayers are being heard. Uncertainty is part of the spiritual journey. However, it is during the darkest moments that faith and prayer can matter the most.

Our prayers may not always be answered in the ways we expect or hope for. However, prayer can be very empowering and healthy. When we are faced with loss, overwhelming burdens, and life-threatening events, then most of us will instinctively turn to a power greater than ourselves. This is when we are at our most authentic and noble. When we express our thoughts and deepest aspirations in prayer, this honest and heartfelt inner dialogue fortifies us to meet life's most formidable challenges.

A good description of what prayer is comes from John Ford's classic film, *How Green Was My Valley*. In the film the narrator and lead character says: "By prayer, I don't mean shouting, mumbling, and wallowing like a hog in religious sentiment. Prayer is only another name for good, clean, direct thinking. When you pray, think. Think well what you're saying. Make your thoughts into things that are solid. In that way, your prayer will have strength, and that strength will become a part of you, body, mind, and spirit."

In other words, prayer is more than just reciting a religious script. Prayer has great power because earnest thought focuses our spiritual energies. Prayer is sincere and mindful thought directed towards a higher power. Prayer is an inner dialogue that aims at truth and understanding. Prayer is an inner conversation, which transforms our heart and soul. Prayer may not be a magic wand, but it can be the beginning of miracles.

Prayer is a way of tapping our spiritual reserves. The root meaning of the word "religion" is *to link back*. In a sense, prayer, like other forms of religious activity, aims at re-connecting us to a transcendent source of meaning and value.

Prayer can help still our minds in troubled times. In particular, praying can also help us cultivate the comfort and calm we need to face the adversity life inevitably throws our way. However, it is also important to pray in good times as well as bad times because prayer can help keep our minds and spirits clear. Perhaps, we should not always expect that our prayers will be answered in the ways we hope for. After all, there is so much in life that is beyond our control. But there is great value in expressing our deepest feelings, hopes, and thoughts in mindful-prayer and meditation. In short, prayer helps us to center our minds and calm our spirits, putting us in touch with something very deep and sincere within us. Discovering and tapping deep reservoirs of inner strength can help us face adversity, surmount challenges, and even accomplish the miraculous.

Living in the Moment

"One of the most tragic things I know about human nature is that all of us tend to put off living. We are all dreaming of some magical rose garden over the horizon – instead of enjoying the roses that are blooming outside our windows today."

-- Dale Carnegie

"The secret of health for both mind and body is not to mourn for the past, not to worry about the future, or not to anticipate troubles, but to live in the present moment wisely and earnestly."

-- Buddha

I am drawing a breath on a sandy beach. As I do, the ocean's waves are brushing up against the shore. The sea is alive and breathing too. It is nighttime and a silver streak of moonlight is dancing on the choppy surface of the water. A gentle breeze ruffles the stillness, but just a tad. My thoughts seem calm and clear. I, and the scene I survey, seem as one.

I am living, breathing, thinking, and feeling in the moment. I have purposively set aside the cares of the day and the concerns of life to marvel at the miracle of a late-night sky. The stars are sparkling in the heavens. Halfluminous clouds drift and unfold slowly from above. I can feel the ebb and flow of the ocean, but the night seems timeless to me.

A few thoughts from the past begin to intrude. I think of loved ones who have completed their voyage on this earth. I feel fondness and gratitude for the moments, the laughter, the joys, and the simple pleasures we shared. The night and the moment seem even more precious to me.

The ability to enjoy the here and now is a tonic for the anxious and care-laden soul. So often, our lives consist of chores, cares, and concerns. Our daily duties and responsibilities are important, but we also need moments when we can lose ourselves to the magic and mysteries of life. Put simply, we all need moments when we can ponder the stunning beauty of the intricate natural order that we are a part of.

Living in the moment is a liberating and refreshing experience. When we live in the here and now it can seem as if we have shed our egos, at least temporarily, and awakened to a more encompassing sense of self. High-achieving athletes, musicians, and creative artists often describe their peak-performances and peak-experiences in similar terms. That is, they speak of letting go of their finite self while tapping into the unconscious (or what they sometimes describe as a higher self).

Absorbing an evening at the ocean like a sponge has left me revitalized. The seemingly eternal stars, the shimmering moonlight, and the respiring sea are now a part of my memory, but they still speak to me. Immersing oneself in nature and the moment is the kind of nourishment every soul needs from time to time.

The Symphony of Life

"My soul is a hidden orchestra; I know not what instruments, what fiddle strings and harps, drums and tamboura I sound and clash inside myself. All I hear is the symphony."

— Fernando Pessoa

There is something about listening to a symphony in a concert hall that makes me appreciate how glorious music can be. The conductor waves his arms and the orchestra responds with a fountain of sound. Musical themes emerge, and then develop, as the composition as a whole unfolds. A great piece of music can take us on a journey through unexpected sonic landscapes, which delight the ear and captivate the imagination.

Music is a uniquely immersive art form. Like the spirit, music is invisible to the eye, but it is nonetheless a very real and potentially transformative phenomenon. The best composers paint pictures with sound. However, their canvas is the listener's imagination.

I love hearing how musical themes develop. A motif is introduced, but it will often recur later in the piece, but with subtle variations. One scholar of music, James Hepokoski, introduced the term "rotational form" to describe how musical themes are transformed within compositions. In his view, musical motifs only assume their true shape, fullest expression, and meaning when they reach the finale that has been the goal of the composition all along.

The idea of the "rotational form" can apply to our lives as well as to music. When the famous philosopher Arthur Schopenhauer reached an advanced age he wrote a work entitled "*On an Apparent Intention in the Fate of the Individual.*" In the essay, he expressed the idea that events and encounters that seemed incidental and random when he was a youth now seemed like themes in a more coherent and orderly story line. It is as if each of our lives is a symphony, but we can only discern the motifs (and their relationship to one another) when we can stand back and appreciate our life in its totality.

We can look at life as a symphony. Nature often seems suffused with broad themes, which surface in a variety of guises. For example, each new morning the sun arises on the horizon from the womb of night. In the afternoon, the sun reaches its peak in the sky. By dusk, however, the sun's light begins to fade. At night, the sun descends below the horizon, only to be reborn the following day.

The seasons can be viewed as a variation on the cyclical motif. Nature blossoms to life in the spring. In the summer, flowers, trees, and vegetation of all sorts are at their most luxuriant. By autumn, leaves turn color and fall from the trees as the bounty of nature seems to wane. During winter, barren branches and cold nights appear to signal that life is in retreat. However, even the bleakest winters cannot extinguish the hope of a new spring.

The human life cycle follows a comparable pattern. Youth, adulthood, middle-age, and old-age resemble the seasons. Furthermore, like the sun itself, we have our sunrise, our peak hour, our sunset years, and a time when our light seems to vanish beneath the horizon.

Each night, our waking self dissolves in the waves of sleep. But every morning our egos are reborn. A sunset, winter, night, and sleep may appear to signal and end of some kind, but they cannot extinguish the promise and hope of rebirth, which is part of the cycle of life. What can appear to be an ending from one vantage point; can seem quite different from the perspective of the cycle as a whole.

Similarly, events in our life (such as the loss of a loved one) will acquire new meanings as we gain the perspective of time. The death of someone we love can seem overbearing at first, but over time painful experiences often yield to bitter sweet memories. Actions we take (such as setting up foundations, charity walks, or creating memorials) will often help transform our perspective on loss. In short, it is up to us to take the pain of loss and turn it into something positive so that we can see things from a richer and deeper perspective.

Death may take our loved ones from us, but it cannot take our treasured memories and the love they shared during their lifetimes. Those memories and the love they shared will forever be a part of us. When the memory of a loved one glows within our heart, then we can find ways to share that light with others. This is one way the departed can continue to have an impact in our world.

The loss of a loved one can tear a hole in the fabric of our lives. However, we can find ways to fill those holes with meaning and with love. In a sense, our days are like the individual threads of a larger tapestry that we spend our lives weaving. If we focus on the individual threads, the elements in a mosaic, or the gaps, then we will be unable to recognize and appreciate things from a deeper vantage point. We need the perspective of time in order to see the larger pattern and the meaning of the mosaic or tapestry as a whole.

It can take considerable time and effort before we can come to terms with the loss of a loved one. It can take a lifetime to transform the pain of a deep loss into something positive. The death of a loved one is undoubtedly a horrific blow that can seem to tear the fabric of our soul. However, given time we can manage to weave the essence of our loved ones into our personal lives so that they become living presences. Composers such as Mozart, Bach, and Vivaldi passed away centuries ago, but the melodies they created continue to inspire and delight the living. Similarly, the essence of our departed loved ones will forever be a part of our experience and who we are. Given the gift of time we can give voice to their spirits, ensuring that they are a part of the symphony of our lives and mankind.

Life is fragile, but life also contains the power to renew itself.

Love and Work

"Love and work are the cornerstones of our Humanness"

-- Sigmund Freud

Love is a blessing that can imbue the world with a sense of the divine. When we are in love our senses seem keener, our lives more meaningful, and the world seems like a better and more hopeful place.

For ages, poets and philosophers have tried to describe and define love. Love is a unifying force, a many-splendored thing, and a gateway to God. Perhaps no description or definition of love will suffice. But I like Plato's likening of love to a ladder, which leads the soul upwards towards the divine.

Love is inexorably tied to forgiveness. There's a wonderful scene in a film called *Into the Wild*, which illustrates how love and forgiveness are intertwined. The film is based on the true story of Christopher McCandless, a gifted young man who abandons his possessions, friends, and his family for a Thoreau-like quest to find a spiritually authentic life in the wilderness. Christopher was a sensitive, appealing, and admirable young person in many ways, but his inability to forgive his parents for normal parental shortcomings led him down the path of social isolation. In the film's most poignant scene Christopher befriends a retired widower, magnificently played by Hal Holbrooke, who gently challenges Christopher's decision to abandon his family. As the retiree so wisely tells Christopher, "when you forgive, you love. And when you love, God's light shines through you."

One day, while attending a memorial service for a friend's mother at a Greek Orthodox Church, I heard a priest deliver a similar message: "when we are estranged from our fellow human beings," he said, "we are estranged from God."

I believe love is the most fundamental force in our lives. Of course, love can take several forms. There is romantic love, sometimes known as *Eros*, which married couples share. As the name implies, erotic love aims at a merger of male and female through sexual union. Also, there is the love between friends, knows as *Philial love*. Philadelphia (the city of brotherly love) derives its name from this form of love. Finally, there is *Agape*, which can refer to the love between God and his creatures, or the feelings of benevolence and charity that humans have for one another.

Love is rooted in desire for completeness. We are all flawed and imperfect creatures. We need to love and be loved in order to thrive and achieve our potential. When we are the beneficiaries of love, we feel a sense of fulfillment and wholeness. Similarly, there is great satisfaction in sharing our light and love with others.

Love is a force that binds couples, families, and communities together. However, when our natural desire to experience love is thwarted, then we can often react in ways that are dysfunctional and self-defeating. Many couples, for instance, try to manipulate one another into getting what they want instead of communicating their needs and desires openly. Good communication (along with trust and respect) is one the most important ingredients in any successful relationship. In particular, being a good listener is essential in any relationship. Indeed, four of the most important words couples can say to one another are: "what are you feeling?"

I like to think of love as a light that makes the world brighter. Of course, excessive ego-centeredness can distort or cloud the light we have to share. Each of us is like a lantern, but our egos can be like the glass panes, which protect the bulb. When the glass panes are speckled with dust, then the light becomes distorted or obscured.

Navigating life requires a healthy ego. But I also believe that the ability to set aside our egos is essential to loving others and accomplishing great things. Many people in today's world think that love is something they are naturally entitled too. However, I believe that love is something that more often than not involves both effort and sacrifice. Often, love can seem elusive and quite challenging, but I prefer to think of love as the most precious gift one can give or receive.

True forms of love lead the soul higher. One of the great tales of love comes from *The Mahabharata,* a classic of Indian literature. The story involves a band of brothers that are engaged on life-long spiritual quest. The brothers are attempting to scale a sacred mountain in the Himalayas, which will lead them to the gates of heaven. Their adventures and trials last many years. Ultimately, only a single brother remains alive to complete their quest. This hero is accompanied by his faithful dog when he reaches the gates of heaven at the top of the mountain.

The hero is greeted by a heavenly gatekeeper, who congratulates him on successfully completing his arduous journey. He tells the hero that the gates of heaven are now open to him and that he will be reunited with his lost brothers and other departed loved ones, but he insists that the hero's dog must remain behind. The hero immediately objects, citing his dog's loyalty and devotion as proof of the dog's worthiness to enter heaven. The heavenly gatekeeper remains insistent that unless the hero abandons his dog he cannot enter paradise.

The hero longs to be reunited with his loved ones, but he cannot bear the thought of abandoning his faithful companion, who is now old and frail. He tells the gatekeeper that it would not be heaven if he were separated from his canine companion and he would prefer to descend the mountain with his dog rather than abandon him. As it happens, the hero's decision to stick with his dog had been his final spiritual test. The gates of heaven were then opened to the hero and his faithful companion.

Love is a unifying and harmonizing power. Love is the force that bridges the gap between individuals. Love is a process that lifts the soul to higher heights. Love can take flawed and broken individuals and make them feel whole. A quote from Victor Hugo's novel *Les Miserable* captures something of the divine nature of love: "To love another person is to see the face of God."

Love is a force that knits individuals together into a larger whole. However, even the strongest bonds can feel frayed at times. The bliss of romantic love can seem heaven sent, but to love deeply is to risk the pain of loss, rejection, and disappointment. Some fortunate few seem to have even-keeled relationships. Most romantic relationships, undoubtedly, will have their ups and downs. But the tests most relationships undergo are not incidental; it is the shared trials of fire that strengthen the bond between couples.

There is a process in physics known as annealing, which bears comparison to the process of love that enduring couples share. In a nutshell, annealing is a method of heating and cooling raw iron so that it becomes tempered steel. A tempered steel blade is far stronger and more durable than a non-tempered blade. Likewise, couples that have weathered the highs and lows of life together often have the strongest bonds. When it comes to couplehood, it is as if life is a crucible in which the elements of our individuality are continually being forged into a more complete and resilient whole.

Most of us want to love and be loved in return. We seek partners who will compliment us, comfort us, and share the joys and sorrows of life with us. Ideally, our partners will help us realize our fullest potential, see us through thick and thin, and nourish us emotionally, physically, and spiritually. Of course, many couples do just the opposite; they seem to bring out the worst in each other.

Relationships are complex and succeeding at them is as much an art as it is a science. However, my sister Anne once mentioned two qualities that are virtually essential for any enduring partnership: 1) trust and 2) respect. If you don't have those two ingredients, then you aren't likely to build a successful relationship.

For centuries, love has been conceptualized as a divine force, which unites couples and leads them towards higher states of mind and being. Undoubtedly, love can seem otherworldly, even heaven sent. But we should also bear in mind that love and illusions often go hand in hand. Love may be divine, but love can also be work. The more we work at it, however, the greater the rewards.

There is something mystical about love. Each of us seeks to be acknowledged, understood, and comforted by our loved ones. But no relationship, no matter how fulfilling, can provide us with all that we seek. Meaningful work is an important component in leading a happy and deeply satisfying life.

One of the most satisfying roles I held was working as a counselor helping disadvantaged youth and adults find the training and employment opportunities, which would allow them to pursue their vocational dreams.

Arriving for work every morning was an energizing experience. It was very gratifying to know I was helping individuals find a job or classroom training that would put them on a more productive and prosperous path.

Helping people thrive has always meant so much to me. Many of the individuals I worked with required a great deal of guidance, attention, and patience. When I helped an individual find a job that gave them self-esteem, dignity, and a steady paycheck, then it made me feel as if a flower I had tended to was blooming. When we have work that we love, then we flower too.

Finding fulfilling work is one of life's greatest challenges. Aristotle believed that "Pleasure in the job puts perfection in the work." That is, when we derive pleasure from what we do, then the end product of our work is more likely to reflect our commitment to excellence. For example, a luthier who loves the process of building guitars is far more likely to build a high quality instrument than a guitar-maker who only cares about making a buck. In short, when we believe in what we do, and when our work is a reflection of who we are, then we feel a justifiable pride in the end product of our labors.

Of course, many jobs are merely a means to an end; supporting ourselves and our families. Worse, some workplaces are demeaning, alienating, and even toxic environments. Too often, the individual can get reduced to being just a cog in the mechanized workplace. Concomitantly, it is very easy to feel irrelevant in the information age. Indeed, finding pleasurable and meaningful work in the modern age is quite a challenge.

However, work is fundamental to the human condition and our sense of dignity. Finding a vocation or career path that matches our interests and skills is one of the most important tasks we face. After all, the occupational, career, or entrepreneurial path we choose will shape our character, help establish our role in society, and provide us with the opportunity to make our mark and leave a legacy.

In many ways, the goals we choose shape who we are. Therefore, we should choose aims and goals that are worthy of our humanity, bring out our best, and express our deepest aspirations.

In choosing a vocation it is important to ask: What are my passions? What do I value? What are the talents and skills I want to express and develop? Transpersonal psychologists introduced the concept of "authenticity" in regards to our social roles. Essentially, an individual who is "true to themselves" is charting their own course and acting according to a deeply held core set of values.

On the other hand, many people bury themselves in a job or a role because they believe that is what others expect of them. Anxiety and a fear of freedom (and the responsibility that goes with it) prompt many people to take jobs that have little meaning for them. Such work may help pay the bills, but it is unlikely to foster happiness (an emotion that arises when we pursue our own special excellence).

To get paid for doing the work you love is one of the greatest pieces of good fortune imaginable. For the vast majority of humanity, work is merely a means to an end: survival. Indeed, more than half of the globe's population gets by on about $2 a day. Those of us who live in affluent societies can be very thankful that we live in environments where there are employment opportunities that allow for self-expression and personal development. It is up to each of us to find – or create – occupational roles which challenge us and allow us to flourish.

Passion, persistence, patience, and perspiration are words we associate with individuals who have achieved occupational or entrepreneurial excellence. It is so important to identify and cultivate our passions. Passions provide us with the motivating energy to accomplish challenging goals. But finding something you love to do is only part of the equation. Becoming good at what you love to do is important, if you want to make a living doing it.

For instance, a person may love playing tennis, but they'll have to practice very hard at it if they are to excel at it. It can take years, even decades, of practice before one becomes an outstanding tennis player. In fact, cognitive scientists suggest that it takes about 10,000 hours of repetitive practice to master any skill or activity (that works out to 3 hours per day for about ten years). That's where persistence, patience, and perspiration come in. Anyone who has risen to the top of their field -- be they a musician, race car driver, athlete, or doctor – has probably invested 10,000 hours of their time practicing and perfecting their skill set. In other words, anyone who is successful has employed the formula of passion, persistence, patience, and perspiration.

Developing and exercising our own special excellences is what leads to happiness. Finding a vocation where we can get paid for doing what we love is a blessing indeed. But simply doing what we love as a hobby is a good thing too. Sometimes, it isn't always possible to find a job or a workplace we enjoy. However, when work becomes monotonous, toxic, or a chore, then it is bound to dampen our spirits. When this happens, having a hobby or activity we can look forward to after work can nourish and sustain us.

It is natural to seek work environments and people that will help us flourish. When our jobs and co-workers do not allow much scope for self-expression and self-discovery, then frustration is likely. However, with the advent of the Internet and the information age it is increasingly possible to find and create new opportunities. As an editorial columnist observes, "If you can't find the job you are looking for, then try and create one."

Love and work are fundamental to the human condition. Each of us hopes to see and realize our ideal selves in our work and in our relationships. However, love and work entail sacrifice and great effort too. Often, we must be prepared to put the needs of our loved one or the goals of an organization ahead of our own. Self-expression and self-realization are important, but sacrifice is an inevitable and often very meaningful part of life. The necessary balancing act between self-realization and sacrifice is expressed in the wonderful Jewish aphorism: "If I am not for myself, then who will be? If I am not for others, then what am I?"

The mythologist Joseph Campbell believed that in choosing a vocation we should "follow our bliss." We should all ask ourselves: "What activity, interest, or field excites our passions and kindles our imagination?" Ideally, the work we choose should challenge us, nourish us, and bring out our best. If a job or workplace environment feels toxic, perpetually frustrating, or demeaning, then it is probably a sign to look into charting a new course. If we allow ourselves to be governed by fear or an excessive prudence when choosing a vocation, then we may find security, but we are unlikely to find happiness. On the other hand, courage, faith in our selves, and a measure of practicality are the qualities likely to help us land the right vocation. Next to choosing a spouse, finding the right kind of work ranks as one of the most important decisions most of us will make. After all, when we find a job that makes us happy, then we are more likely to make our significant others contented too. To quote Charles Pratt: "Be true to your work and your work will be true to you." This is a recipe for a happy and fulfilling life.

Surmounting Fear

"A life lived in fear is half lived."

-- Spanish proverb

"Adversity is the mother of progress."

-- Gandhi

"I ask not for a lighter burden, but for broader shoulders."

-- Jewish Proverb

Erik Weihenmayer is an accomplished mountaineer who has scaled some of the world's highest peaks, including Everest. Erik's climbing feats are remarkable by any standard. But the fact that Erik is blind makes his accomplishments even more impressive and inspiring. Erik lost his sight in college, but rather than curse his fate, like many of us might, he embraced his adversity. As a result, he transformed disability into opportunity. After all, as he acknowledges in his motivational lectures, it is unlikely he would have taken up the dangerous and demanding path of mountaineering were it not for his vision loss.

Christopher Reeve was one of the most handsome and appealing actors of his generation. Tall, well-built, and exceptionally athletic, Reeve seemed the ideal choice to play "Superman," the role that launched him to superstardom. Tragically, Reeve was paralyzed from the neck down following a freak horseback riding accident. However, despite being confined to a wheel chair and dependent on a respirator, Reeve managed to direct films, star in movies, lobby on behalf of the disabled, and author his autobiography. In short, Reeve managed to accomplish more in his life after his accident than most able-bodied individuals achieve in their entire lifetimes.

Les Paul was one of the most important musical figures of the 20th century. He was an accomplished guitarist and a best-selling artist. But he also single-handedly invented the electric guitar and multi-track recording, two developments that revolutionized the music industry. In his later years, the onset of arthritis threatened Les Pauls's high standard of play. However, Les Paul adapted his technique, which allowed him to perform live regularly well into his nineties.

Weihenmayer, Reeve, and Les Paul all share one thing in common: they faced great adversity, but the human spirit in them glowed brighter as they overcame the obstacles they encountered. Many of us seek to avoid adversity. However, the accomplishment of numerous exceptional men and women illustrate that adversity and spiritual growth often go hand in hand.   It is natural to fear many of the misfortunes and hardships life presents. But fear of living can actually be one of the biggest impediments to leading a fulfilling life.

The failure to live fully can engender self-destructive tendencies. We are creatures which naturally seek happiness, self-expression, and the joys and adventures life can offer. To find these, however, means taking risks. If we shirk risk, then energy and attention which is focused outward towards the flow of life can instead end up being bottled-up inside us in ways that can lead to anxiety and depression.

We are creatures that naturally seek to transcend ourselves and our circumstances. Life has a way of throwing many obstacles in our path, but there is something energizing about setting ambitious goals and trying to accomplish them. There is also something very enlivening about living fully and savoring every moment. Yes, tears and adversity are an inescapable part of life, but overcoming challenges can bring out our best.

Undoubtedly, life's burdens can seem overwhelming at times. But life is filled with great joy, beauty, and many wonderful things too. It is up to us to make the most of every moment we are given. If you are unhappy, then try and put a smile on someone else's face. If you are depressed, then try and set a worthy goal that will put you on a new and brighter path. If you find yourself fearful, then summon up some courage by trying to do something that challenges you to go beyond yourself. Ultimately, it is by pushing ourselves beyond our limits that we find our truest selves. That is when we feel most alive.

Thoughts on Friendship

"A friendship is a single soul dwelling in two bodies."

-- Aristotle

"And in the sweetness of friendship let there be laughter, and sharing of pleasures. For in the dew of little things the heart finds its morning and is refreshed."

-- Kahlil Gibran

I am talking with my childhood friend Eileen about our summers on the Jersey shore. I catch a mischievous twinkle in her eye, a knowing smile, and a sly inflection of humor in her voice. We both share a subtle understanding beyond words. We are not just having a discussion; we have entered into a dialogue, which makes both of us feel like a genuinely soulful exchange is taking place.

Being recognized as a unique individual is a precious experience. Many friendships, relationships, and encounters can seem transactional (that is, they are of the "I'll scratch your back if you'll scratch my back" type). However, I believe that we all have a deep longing to be acknowledged and appreciated, not just as a means for somebody else's end, but for who we are in and of ourselves.

It is natural to want to enjoy the company of friends. Ideally, we want to see our friends thrive and to help them when we can. Seeing a friend succeeding or flourishing puts a smile on my face. On the other hand, when a friend faces setbacks, depression, or loss, then I am saddened too.

Sharing simple joys with a friend can be one of life's greatest pleasures. Sharing a true friend's burdens can be deeply meaningful too. Friends can be of enormous comfort to us when we face loss. Seeing familiar faces, hearing kind words, and experiencing empathy can help lift our spirits when they are at their lowest and provide a sense of normalcy.

Reciprocity is essential to friendship. Most of us have experienced "fair weather friends," acquaintances who are full of goodwill and good intentions when times are easy, but who never seem to come through in a pinch. One can never have enough true friends. But it is worth remembering that real friends are hard to come by.

Helen Keller once said that "walking with a friend in the dark is better than walking alone in the light." Sharing the simple joys and pleasures of life with friends is to be treasured, but true friends will be there to share the burdens, disappointments, and sad moments too. It may sound like a simple concept, but to have a friend you must also be a friend.

In a nutshell, being there for one another is what friendship is all about. I met three of my closest friends –

Anne, Clare, and Kathi – more than thirty-five years ago while attending Merrimack College. Over the years, my college roommates (as I still refer to them) and I have enjoyed some great times together. But we've also never missed a wedding, a funeral, or other important life events. If there's one lesson I live by it is this: friends make time for each other.

For more than three decades and counting my college roommates and I have set aside one weekend a year for an annual reunion. It is a time to reminisce, enjoy each other's company, and to celebrate accomplishments and life's milestones. It's a simple custom, but an exceptionally meaningful one, which has nurtured, strengthened, and deepened the bonds between us.

Memories created with friends have a special radiance. I have many fond reminiscences of paling around with my grade school friends, Mary and Val. We rode our bikes, played tag, ice-skated, and explored our little hometown. We were adventurous, and many times found ourselves climbing in the newly constructed homes, where we left our handprints in the wet cement floors. Today, more than forty years later, we still remain the closest of friends. Our strong bond of friendship has helped soften our despair following loss and we continue to depend on each other during our darkest moments. Reflecting on my childhood, I realize that my friends and I left more than our handprints in the wet cement. As our friendship continues to solidify I find that the deepest and most

lasting impression is the one we have made upon each
other; we have imprinted ourselves in each other's hearts

Friends become part of who we are. We share each other's
happiness, sorrows, and important life events. The values
that my friends exemplify – trust, loyalty, and generosity –
are etched in my soul. The qualities my friends exhibit –
warmth, kindness, and understanding – are embedded in
my heart. The moments we have shared are imprinted in
the essence of my very being. A friend is a present you
give to yourself. Their presence in my life is invaluable.
With a true friend; the more you give the more you receive
in return. Recently, my friend Val and her husband Tony
gave me a coffee mug emblazoned with the lyrics from a
song by *The Beatles*: "I Get By With A Little Help From My
Friends." Those words sum up the value and importance
of friendship so well. We do all indeed get by with a little
help from our friends.

Friends help friends get by. They lighten the load by
sharing burdens. They can help put a smile on our face
when things seem gloomy. Their small gestures and
kindness can restore our hope. The care and
thoughtfulness they display towards us in difficult times
can mean more to us than words can express. I'll never
forget, for instance, the support my friend Cathy provided
me shortly after my mom suffered a heart attack. At the
time, I was my mother's primary caregiver, but Cathy (who
is also a nurse) volunteered to help me as I looked after my
mother. I will be forever touched by the compassion and

selflessness Cathy showed. During one of the most challenging times in my life Cathy was truly "my angel on earth."

Following the Golden Rule is one of the best ways to meet and keep friends. Treating people the way you would want to be treated is one of the simplest and most reliable ways to make and build friendships. Invariably, mutual respect, trust, and empathy are at the heart of any enduring friendship. A true friendship is one of the greatest blessings in life. After all, it is the true friend who is like the ray of sunshine that warms our hearts and helps us to flourish.

Overcoming Depression

"There are wounds that never show on the body that are
deeper and more hurtful than anything that bleeds."

-- Laurell K. Hamilton

Depression is like a hazy fog which clouds our view and
obstructs us from moving forward in life. When we are
depressed we feel weighed down by the troubles of life.
Often, we irrationally convince ourselves that our
circumstances will never change. Depression can be a
natural response to the tragedies, injustices, and burdens
that all of us must face. However, when feelings of
depression fail to lift or dissipate over time, then we are
dealing with more than just an ordinary case of the blues.

Depression can have many causes. Indeed, depression is
very often a natural and entirely understandable response
to the misfortunes, setbacks, and disappointments we all
will encounter in life. Depression has a way of feeding on
itself, however. When we are depressed we often feel
incapable of taking action that might lift us out of the
doldrums. In this way, depression can easily become a
vicious cycle that feeds on itself.

Enduring depression is not without its rewards. As the
poet John Keats, for instance, once noted: "Do you not see

how necessary a world of pains and troubles is to school an intelligence and make it a soul?" Indeed, passing through a process known as "the dark night of the soul" can help forge a stronger, deeper, and more empathetic personality. However, we must be careful not to romanticize depression too much. Yes, depression is often linked to exceptional creativity, but most depressive episodes lead nowhere.

Every depression is unique. Yet, arguably there is a common thread running through virtually all depressions; an acute preoccupation, recognition of, or focus on the suffering of one's self. Ironically, some forms of therapy may actually reinforce the acute sense of self-awareness that is often associated with depression. If an acute sense of self is often at the root of depression, then perhaps finding ways to lose one's self might mitigate depression.

As it happens, losing one's sense of self is characteristic of peak experiences, a psychological state that is the polar opposite of depression. For instance, star athletes often talk about losing their sense of self during the process of exceptional athletic performances. Likewise, musicians and artists frequently describe being outside of themselves during a particularly brilliant performance or the creative process.

Finding healthy ways to at least temporarily shed our sense of self may help alleviate depression. Volunteering, taking up an athletic activity, or finding a hobby are simple ways of shifting the focus away from ourselves and our cares.

Expectations are another factor related to depression. If you are meeting with your boss and are expecting to get a raise, but you instead get fired, then you will be far more depressed than if you did not expect a raise in the first place. To paraphrase the psychologist William James, there is nothing so painful as an erroneous expectation or a false belief. Adjusting our expectations so that they are more in line with what reality has to offer can save us from a lot of grief. Of course, a great deal of human progress is made by idealists and optimists who refuse to lower their expectations or settle for "reality." Nevertheless, we need to be aware how expectations and beliefs influence our moods.

The word "depression" conjures up an image of something pressing down upon us, squeezing the life out of us. An antonym for the word depression might be "enthusiasm," which etymologically speaking means "to be filled with the gods." With depression, it seems our energy spirals inward until we feel our spirits crushed. On the other hand, with enthusiasm our energies seem directed outward towards people, tasks, activities, and things beyond ourselves.

We all have a natural inclination to be creative, to express ourselves, and to live fully. When we suppress our appetite for life, however, then our instinct for life can become misdirected, pent up, and ultimately self-destructive. The failure to channel our energies into living fully can manifest as depression or other self-destructive tendencies.

Society often encourages us to defer gratification or substitute trivial pleasures for real life. How many of us spend our days planning for the future and our evenings watching television? However, life is all around us, here and now, and it is up to us to seize the moment, live fully, and make the most of every day. Sometimes, it takes a bit of daring to break out of our routine to see a show, visit an amusement park, or enjoy an unplanned picnic. Yet, spontaneity is the essence of soulfulness.

There is a wonderful scene in the movie *Zorba the Greek*, which illustrates the importance of spontaneity. In the film a prim, proper, and intellectual character (played by the actor Alan Bates) has seen all his hard work, plans and ambitions come to nothing. In a fit of exasperation he asks his friend, Zorba (played Anthony Quinn), to teach him to dance as the two share a bottle of wine on the beach. This is the kind of spontaneous moment Zorba lives for. Life may have confounded their deepest aspirations, but they can still enjoy a fabulous evening dancing on the sands of the ocean. We would do well to cultivate a similar attitude. Life has a way of confounding our expectations, but we can still wrest moments of happiness, joy, and bliss if we are willing to go with the flow and be spontaneous. Remember, if we make an effort to try and see beyond the clouds of grief and depression, then there is always the promise of light up ahead.

The Birth of the Mind

"Out of a misty dream our path emerges for awhile, then closes within a dream."

-- Ernest Dawson

"Dare to live the life you have dreamed for yourself. Go forward and make your dreams come true."

-- Ralph Waldo Emerson

Our early ancestors, prehistoric cave dwellers buried their dead. No one can say with certainty when the practice of ritual burial began, but anthropologists believe that the custom goes back at least 100,000 years.

The cave artwork painted by our ancient ancestors still astounds. Equally affecting is evidence of early grave sites filled with not only skeletal remains, but also tools and sacramental artifacts. The origin of our species, the birth of the human mind, and an awareness of death are all intertwined.

One can imagine that the first tears shed were for the death of a loved one. Tools and other artifacts buried along with the dead suggest that our earliest ancestors believed in an afterlife. For example, the hunter of the clan would need the spear buried next to him in the next world.

Our species has come a long way in terms of technology since prehistoric times. But in many ways our view of death is probably remarkably similar. We tremble at the finality of death and the prospect of losing our loved ones. We also seek ways to revere those who have passed on and we find solace in remembering their deeds and the way those closest to us have touched our lives. Instinctively, we act according to the belief that the individual transcends the physical.

Death remains an awe-inspiring mystery. Humans have tried to find words to describe Death – Death is a "thief," a "liberator," even an "undiscovered country from which no traveler has returned" – but it is a subject that remains shrouded and beyond the ken of all the living.

The filmmaker/comedian Woody Allen once quipped that he didn't mind the prospect of death, but he just didn't want to be there when it happened. Allen's joke gets at something important. After all, most of us naturally try to avoid the subject of death, as if it were something that only happens to others.

Death, however, is an inextricable part of life. In a real sense, life is made more precious and more meaningful because of the fact of death. We can choose to fill each moment we have with love, creative acts, and a sense of purpose. When we live fully and with zest each moment becomes a potential gift. Conversely, squandering our time on earth and cursing our fate can breed a sense of anomie and feelings of depression. Each moment is potentially unique and will never be repeated. The philosopher Socrates once said "the unexamined life is not worth living." But perhaps it would be truer to say that it is "the unlived life that is not worth living." That is, the more fully we embrace life the more meaningful and precious it becomes.

The unlived life is one of life's greatest tragedies. We justly celebrate the life of someone who has lived fully and passed away at a ripe old age. Attaining a measure of wisdom, happiness, and dying without regrets is something we should all aspire to. Unfortunately, many of us fail to take advantage of and appreciate the opportunities life offers us. To be sure, life is by no means easy. But there is something to be said for the mythologist Joseph Campbell's advice that it is the task of heroes and heroines "to participate joyfully in the sorrows of life."

There is a story that illustrates something important about the human condition. According to this tale a Zen monk is walking along the edge of an isolated cliff. He accidently falls over the side, but he manages to catch hold of a small bush branch protruding from a narrow ledge, which is also home to a beautiful flower. The monk, dangling from the narrow ledge, knows he cannot climb up the cliff to save himself, but he also realizes he cannot cling to the bush's branch forever. Instead of expending energy worrying about his impending death, or engaging in a futile effort to save himself, the monk simply concentrates his awareness on the beauty of the flower.

Shakespeare once wrote: "We are such stuff as dreams are made on/and our little life is rounded with a sleep." Throughout history, humans have drawn comparisons between sleep and death. For example, sleep has been described as "the sister of death." This figure of speech is worth pondering. For example, each night our consciousness is extinguished in sleep, only to be reborn the following day. The psychologist Carl Jung believed that the sleep/waking cycle pointed towards a symbolic truth about life. Each night our consciousness "drowns" in the waves of sleep, only to resurface the following day. In a sense, our waking self "dies" each evening, but a night's sleep is not really the end of our consciousness. Similarly, the death of the body may appear to be a final horizon, but perhaps it is a natural progression in a cycle that includes a spiritual rebirth.

Shakespeare insisted that all authentic power derives from dreams. However, so many dreams seem like fragmentary, indecipherable nonsense. Nevertheless, every now and then an uncanny dream arises which perplexes the mind and grips the imagination. I had one such dream several years ago. One morning, lying suspended between the shadows of the night and the sun's radiance, I dreamt I was hovering over an immense graveyard. Slabs of granite extended infinitely in every direction amidst a desolate field. Strangely, the silent stone markers lay horizontally flat against the earth.   Out of curiosity, I drew closer to the plots below.   As I did, the colorless headstones came to life, flickering with brightly-colored images reflecting the lives of our departed fellow travelers.   Each marble mirror was a story filled with hope, suffering, and love. I was overcome with an immense feeling of empathy as I awakened to the feeling of sunlight streaming gently across my cheek. It felt good to be alive and to have the opportunity to add to the human story.

Memories and the Soul

"Death leaves a heartache no one can heal, love leaves a memory no one can steal."

-- Irish Gravestone

"You would not find the boundaries of the soul no matter how many paths you traveled, so deep is its measure."

-- Heraclitus

The opening of John Ford's film, *How Green Was My Valley*, always touches my heart. The narrator, recalling his departed loved ones asks: "Can I believe my friends all gone when their voices are still a glory in my ears. No, and I will stand to say no and no again for they remain a living truth within my mind."

Every now and again, I have an uncanny sense that one of my departed loved ones is with me. Sometimes I feel their presence. Other times I have the feeling that I am looking at things through their eyes. I cannot prove my intuition, of course, but I also believe I should not ignore or discard feelings that seem so palpably real.

I have lost four family members, but the light, love, and values they shared remain as real and indelible to me as anything in this life. I view my sister Pat, my brother Jim, my mom, and my dad, not just as bright spots in my memory, but as living essences implanted in my soul.

Douglas Hofstadter, a Pulitzer Prize winning author has a similar outlook. In 1993, Hofstadter's wife, Carol, passed away suddenly of an undiagnosed brain tumor while the couple was on vacation. Carol left behind two young children and a heartbroken husband. Hofstadter provides a moving account of how deeply his wife's death affected him in his book *Le Ton Beau De Marot: In Praise of the Music of Language,* which is both a tribute to his wife and a scholarly work.

According to Hofstadter, our loved ones can imprint themselves upon us to such an extent that they become part of who we are. When we live with someone long enough, when we come to know them deeply, then we can come to anticipate how they think and feel. To a certain extent, we can even absorb their point of view. Long-married couples, for instance, can often finish each other's sentences and anticipate each other's thoughts.

When our loved ones leave an impression on us we are in fact incorporating part of their essence. That is, our loved ones can literally become part of us. This view has some rather astounding implications. It suggests are loved ones are always with us.

This point was brought home to me recently following an annual family house crawl. Each year, our family sets aside one day for a family event where we partake of food and drink at each other's houses. We enjoy about an hour of socializing at each house before walking as a group to the next house. We have special t-shirts made up for the occasion, with the initials of our departed loved ones inscribed on the shoulder.

The house crawl is an occasion when our entire family joins together to celebrate as one. It is a day of merriment and commemoration. I know my mom and dad would be so happy to see us celebrating together; to them, family was the most important thing in the world. During the day, I overheard several of my nieces and nephews expressing just how important family was to them. It was wonderful to see the seeds my mom and dad planted were now flourishing. Immediately, I felt that the values and ideals my mom and dad lived by were now living on in their descendants. It was if part of my mom and dad were ingrained in my nieces and nephews.

Seeing the world through the eyes of a loved one, it seems to me, is like sharing part of their soul. For instance, when I read one of Emily Dickenson's poems, I sometimes imagine that I am seeing the world through her eyes. To a certain extent I am, since the words she wrote do reflect something of her essence. Likewise, listening to one of Mozart's sublime melodies provides me with a window into his genius.

Mozart's music, like the poems of Emily Dickenson, or the works of other great artists, lives on eternally in the minds and hearts of receptive individuals. But it is not just the famous and exceptional men and women who make deep and lasting impressions. All those who have touched our lives have etched their essence into our memories and souls. The departed can no longer give voice to their stories. It is up to us to tell their stories for them. We can still share something of their soul with others, for their essence is a part of us.

When we share ourselves and our perspective with a receptive other then we are implanting a part of our self in another, and vice versa. We can live in others, just as others can live in us. The boundaries of our souls are indeed beyond all measure.

The Power of Love

"The best and most beautiful things in the world cannot be seen or even touched. They must be felt with the heart"

– Helen Keller

Sometime ago, I was out for a country stroll. The sun was shining, the air was clear, and the day had a timeless feel. After walking some miles I encountered a spry woman in her mid-nineties scurrying to her mail box. Her voice radiated happiness as she exclaimed "hello." We struck up a conversation and I was immediately impressed with her energy, vigor, and her evident enthusiasm for life. Before we parted ways I asked her what the secret was to her apparent youthfulness? "I just love everybody and everything," she replied. It was an answer so simple and beautiful that I felt my spirit instantly aligned itself to the deeper harmony that governs the universe.

Some people are like supernovas; they radiate light and goodness. Unfortunately, some people can be like black holes; they can suck the life and vitality out of all that comes within their orbit. In my experience, it is people who know how to love who find lasting happiness. Conversely, those who consistently act selfishly and put their own egos ahead of others only succeed in making themselves and others miserable over the long term.

When the folk guitar legend Doc Watson passed away a musicologist summed up his legacy in just two words: pure love. Watson was blind since childhood, but he envisioned a style of playing that revolutionized the guitar world. However, it is the sheer joy and enthusiasm Watson imbues his songs with that captivates, amazes, and inspires listeners. Watson could have easily begrudged his fate. Instead, he poured his heart and soul into his music. As a result, he became a musical beacon that continues to shine long after his death.

There is something steadfast and enduring about love. It is the same with the truth. Truth can be viewed as the glue that keeps relationships, families, and society together. On the other hand, we can think of lies as steroids. Lies can confer temporary advantages, but ultimately pervasive lies undermine the foundations of our institutions, be they marriages, families, or companies. For example, the tale of Pinocchio may seem like a simple childhood fable, but his story illustrates a deep psychological truth about lying. Pinocchio is a puppet who dreams of being a real boy. However, he has a tendency to exaggerate and tell fibs, particularly when he is under stress. The more lies he tells, however, the longer his nose grows. Similarly, as a general rule the more we veer from the truth, the more our problems tend to grow. Like Pinocchio, we often lie to reduce anxiety. However, over the long term we undermine our identity, increase our anxiety, and multiply our problems when we are untruthful. Indeed, there is great wisdom in Walter Scott's insight: "Oh! What a tangled web we weave, when we first practice to deceive!"

There is something about beauty that nourishes the soul. A spellbinding sunset, a glorious patch of flowers, and a limpid melody can fill us with a sense of wonder and gratitude. When we are fortunate enough to glimpse the aesthetic dimension of creation we can feel deeply attuned to the universe.

The philosopher Plato believed that contemplating beautiful things made the soul beautiful. In his view, a worldly example of beauty was but an imperfect copy of a spiritual form of beauty. However, to contemplate and reflect on worldly beauty prepared the soul on its upward journey towards the spiritual realm. For Plato, examples of earthly beauty were like the steps on the ladder of love, which led the soul ever higher.

Love is the principle associated with transcendence. By pouring his or her soul into their work the artist, composer, or architect creates art forms that transcend time and place. Similarly, the love between a husband and wife that culminates in sexual union leads to a new generation, which transcends the original couple. Love, indeed, is the power that takes us beyond ourselves.

Surely, if there is any force that can overcome the sting of death, it is love. There is a wonderful ballad, called "Turn of the Century," by the rock group Yes, which illustrates how love can help us cope with the pain of losing a loved one. "Turn of the Century" tells the story of an artist who loses the love of his life to illness, but he recreates her beauty in a statute that seems to come to life. The song is an affirmation of the artist's ability to transform pain and loss into a work of beauty. Sometimes life deals us tragic blows. We can respond to these blows with rage, or we can try and respond constructively with love. Obviously, the latter path is very difficult, but transforming pain into something positive does represent a triumph of the human spirit.

Love is both a choice and an act of creation. It is only human nature when we respond to death with fear, anger, or denial. We are frail creatures, after all, and the death of a loved one (or of ourselves) can be a terrifying prospect we naturally hope to avoid. There is something divine, however, when we manage to transform our pain into acts of kindness and love. We cannot eliminate the void that is left in death's wake, but we can fill it with gestures, rituals, and works that make the world a better place.

Transcending our circumstances is never easy. But the motif of life overcoming itself does seem to be a recurrent theme in nature. Think of the snake that sheds its skin, the couple that lives on through their children, or the caterpillar, which sheds its cocoon in the process of becoming a butterfly. In the sense, the caterpillar dies, but in doing so it becomes a new form of life, a butterfly, which can spread its wings as it soars on an invisible wind. Perhaps the image of a caterpillar being reborn as a butterfly contains a poetic truth: what seems like the end can, in fact, be a new beginning.

Sacred Places and Sacred Time

The idea of a sacred place...is apparently as old as life itself."

-- Joseph Campbell

"There are...places where one breathes in spirit, places where a man can steep himself in it, or if you prefer, where he quickens the sense of the divine in himself. This is the greatest gift of Earth and Heaven to man."

-- Louis Charpentier

"Man does not weave the web of life; he is merely a strand in it."

-- Chief Seattle

Years ago, I was exploring the countryside in Ireland. Unexpectedly, I came across a desolate field near the farmhouse where I was staying. In the distance I spied a small plot of shrubs and tall weeds surrounded by a dilapidated enclosure. As I moved closer I noticed a few dozen tall stone monoliths jutting out from amongst the vegetation. Many of the inscriptions on the graveyard markers had been rendered illegible by time and the elements. But from what I could make out, many of the graves dated back eight centuries or more. I was filled with a sense of awe, reverence, and timelessness. I keenly felt I had discovered a sacred place, which made me feel that I was connected to my ancestors, humanity, and the mysterious forces of life.

We are creatures that instinctively seek meaning, purpose, and to know our place in the scheme of things. In today's modern world, however, it is increasingly hard to find firm ground and a fixed point of reference. For example, often institutions and traditions no longer seem capable of answering all of life's questions or offering infallible moral and metaphysical guidance. Increasingly, individuals can find themselves adrift in a sea of secular uncertainty with no safe harbor for the soul in sight.

In times such as these, it is more important than ever to seek out sacred places and carve out sacred time. Etymologically speaking, the word "sacred" means "to make holy." Holy, of course is a virtual homophone of the word "whole." Indeed, one could argue that one function of sacred places is to help make an individual feel psychologically and spiritually whole.

Humans have been setting aside sacred places and carving out time since the dawn of mankind. In essence, a sacred place (or sacred time) is a point of intersection between the human and the divine. A sacred place can be a church, a temple, synagogue, mosque, cemetery, historical site, or a site created for the purpose of communing with a transcendent source or power. Sacred times are akin to sacred places, though they are marked on calendars rather than on geographical maps.

One purpose of a sacred site or time is to orient individuals to a transcendent dimension. Presumably, there is something about the human condition which has made sacred places something of a necessity.

Ideally, sacred places should help individuals focus and deepen their attention towards matters of ultimate concern. Today, so much of our time in the secular world is spent on practical, mundane, and often trivial matters. Sacred sites are a reminder that life is not just about fulfilling our physical needs; we also have spiritual concerns related to meaning, purpose, and questions of ultimate value. We look at spiritual sites as places where we can feel the mystery of life and reflect on its importance for us and our loved ones.

Sacred places can be sites where individuals come together. Or the individual can create their own sacred place (or carve out their own sacred time) where they pray, meditate, perform religious rituals, or simply commune with a higher power or core self. The important thing is that a sacred place should be a site that pitches our consciousness towards the spiritual dimension of life and away from worldly matters.

The demands of modern life are incessant. Many of us cope with stressful workplaces, family demands, and a seemingly never-ending blizzard of bills and responsibilities. A secularized public square, and the sometimes mundane nature of existence, can sap our spirits. Finding or creating a sacred place, however, can put us in touch with the poetic, mystical, and spiritual dimensions of life. Put simply, even a few minutes a day in a sacred place can refresh our spirits and give us the fortitude to face our worldly challenges. A sacred place can be as simple as a prayer mat, a room with a candle, and/or a room where we can perform a small ritual aimed at centering and concentrating our minds on the spiritual aspects of life. Of course, many of us will gravitate towards traditional sacred spaces, such as houses of worship, as the sites most conducive to awakening our spiritual potential. However, for others a park bench, a garden, or quiet spot in nature may help one tap into and concentrate one's spiritual energies. The important thing is to find or create a sacred space that we can visit regularly so that we can pray, reflect, commune with a higher power, and experience the spiritual aspects of life.

For some, a sacred place is no more than a figment of the imagination. There may be some truth in that. It is through the power of imagination that some places do become meaningful and even sacred for us. However, we should not underestimate or dismiss the importance of the imagination in its sincerest and most constructive form. Humanity's greatest artists – Mozart, Leonardo da Vinci, and Michelangelo, for example – tapped their imaginations and gave voice to our deepest aspirations. In doing so, they created works that expressed the highest potential of the human spirit. In short, they created sacred art.

As the French writer Joseph Joubert noted, "Imagination is the eye of the soul." We need spaces where we can give voice to our deepest aspirations and allow our minds to be transported out of the mundane and into the poetic and spiritual dimensions of life. Sacred places provide a place where we can ponder the mysteries of life and think and feel clearly about matters of ultimate importance. Today, when the social order and traditional institutions seem to be fragmenting, it is more important than ever for individuals to find and create scared places where they can get centered and summon the strength to meet life's daily challenges.

Responding to Loss with Love

"If you change the way you look at things, the things you look at change."

-- Wayne Dyer

"Bad things do happen; how I respond to them defines my character and the quality of my life. I can choose to sit in perpetual sadness, immobilized by the gravity of my loss, or I can choose to rise from the pain and treasure the most precious gift I have – life itself."

-- Walter Anderson

Life can be overwhelming at times. Indeed, sometimes the world can seem like an unfriendly and inhospitable place. Life has a way of testing all of us and every spiritual journey is bound to include a phase referred to as "the dark night of the soul."

For the Swiss psychologist, Carl Jung, the human mind was like a candle in the night. In his view, the universe would remain a dark and unaware landscape without the light of human consciousness to illuminate it. When you think of it, consciousness is both a gift and burden. As conscious creatures we have the capacity to savor the joys and beauties of the world, but we are also acutely aware of our mortality and the sting of death.

The flame each of us carries is vitally important because we have the potential to brighten the world we live in. Sometimes, the spark of consciousness we carry inside of us can seem small or insignificant compared to the world we dwell in. But it is worth remembering: the light from a single candle is even more precious when the world is at its darkest.

Consciousness is inherently creative. The world we experience is a product of both our mind and the universe that we inhabit. Each sunset, each meal, and every personal encounter is a potentially unique experience which will never be repeated. As conscious creatures we can make choices. We can embrace experience with a zest for life in order to maximize its pleasures and rewards, or we can adopt an attitude of detachment in order to try and mitigate its sorrows.

Many of the events that befall us are entirely beyond our control. However, our freedom consists in how we choose to respond to events. We can respond to setbacks and loss by reacting with anger, or we can try and channel our energies in constructive ways. Invariably, a situation is what it is, but we do have a choice in how we deal with events and what they mean for us.

The loss of a loved one is undoubtedly the ultimate blow. It is natural that we should be angry, despondent, and shaken to our core. Often, we target our emotional rage at life, God, or even ourselves. The grieving process can be lengthy and precarious. Most of us are far too flawed to respond constructively and ideally to all of the misfortunes life can mete out. However, ultimately finding a way to focus our energies into acts of love is in our interest. Remaining angry and depressed over a loss will stunt our growth and corrode our souls. Conversely, finding ways to respond to our loss with love can help both us and our fellow travelers to flourish.

Virtually each and every one of us will face great adversity, disappointment, and loss in our lives. Most of us will face physical and psychological suffering too. Realizing this fact, it makes sense to try and show kindness to others when we can. Being kind to others not only lightens the load of our fellow travelers; we also help ourselves when we help others. When we recognize and appreciate the plight of others, and take steps to mitigate their suffering, then we take the focus away from ourselves. If we are less preoccupied with ourselves and our problems, then we are more apt to feel happy.

Einstein once asked: "Is the universe friendly?" This is a very profound question. Does the universe care about us? Is reality completely indifferent to our fate and suffering? Is nature populated by egoistic creatures pursuing their own interests? Human beings and many other mammals do seem motivated by empathy, compassion, and altruism. Elephants appear to mourn their dead. Comfort dogs and cats appear to sense when hospice residents are nearing the end of their days. And humans often make great personal sacrifices to help complete strangers. Yes, there are plenty of self-absorbed and selfish individuals out there, but there is a good deal of altruism too.

We need to have a healthy regard for ourselves and our own interests. But recognizing and serving the interests of others can make us happier and healthier too. After all, studies show that people who volunteer, pray for others, and perform altruistic acts derive numerous health benefits. In other words, helping others to thrive can help us flourish too.

We may not be able to answer Einstein's question ("Is the universe friendly?") definitively. However, we can do our part to make the universe a friendlier place. By putting our heart and soul into things, by acting out of love, we can brighten the world and make it a more hopeful and beautiful place. Often, the world can seem like a dark realm. The shadows of death and suffering can for a time dim our spirits and obscure the beauty that surrounds us. The light of consciousness each of us has may seem insignificant in the scheme of things. However, the light from one candle can be used to light countless other flames. We cannot expunge death and darkness from our world, but together we can make the world a brighter place.

Sunflowers and the Aim of Life

"Nature does nothing in vain."

-- Aristotle

"Eternity is in love with the productions of times."

-- William Blake

There is something about the sunflower that captures my imagination; the beautiful yellow petals, which unfold so gracefully at the periphery of the flower, the symmetrical swirl of seeds in the center, and the entire plant orienting itself towards the sun. The ancient Greek philosopher Plato believed that the Sun was the visible manifestation of the principle of Goodness, which is a close analogue to the concept of God.

The sun, of course, is a source of light and nourishment for all things. Historically, the sun has been associated with morality, spirituality, and the divine. Our ancient ancestors oriented their lives towards the sun. We may no longer worship the sun, as our ancestors once did, but the sun is indispensible to life.

The interrelationship between a sunflower and the sun reflects an extraordinary natural intelligence. Each morning, the sunflower unfolds its symmetrical golden petals to capture the sun's rays. The sun's energy causes the sunflower to grow and produce the seeds of the next generation. The aim of the sunflower seed is to become a sunflower plant. And the aim of the sunflower plant is to harness the sun's rays so that it may flourish.

Like the sunflower, which orients itself to the sun, we humans orient ourselves to a moral and spiritual horizon. In many ways, the sun is a living symbol of life's goodness. The sun illuminates our world, provides warmth, and nourishes all things. A sunrise signals the start of a fresh new day, and the radiance of the sun as it peers over the horizon provides feelings of hope and a fresh beginning. The importance of the sun as a spiritual metaphor is illustrated by the way we use the word *sun* in language. For instance, we often speak of someone positive as having a *sunny disposition*. Conversely, we often refer to the *haze of depression* or the *clouds of sadness*.

My brother Jim was like a ray of sunshine; he was always brightening people's lives. He was a natural comedian and his radiant personality seemed to lift the spirits of everyone he encountered. As one friend noted, "Jim just illuminated every room he came into." Some people are just like that, they seem to embody the goodness and bounty of life.

The smile on the face of a friend or loved one, a glorious sunrise, or the way multi-colored flowers glisten in the sunshine can remind us of how much beauty there is in the world. There is a Navajo prayer that goes like this: *In beauty I walk. With beauty before me, I walk. With beauty behind me, I walk. With beauty below me, I walk. With beauty above me, I walk. With beauty all around me, I walk.*

I was in Ireland recently hiking along the northern coast. Every which way I turned seemed more beautiful than the next. Rolling hills, carpeted in green, stretched as far as the eyes could see. Majestic cliffs, dotted with colorful wildflowers, jutted up from the ocean. A translucent sea brushed up against the shore while sunlight sparkled on the water's surface. Volcanic rock, which had naturally formed into hexagonal patterns eons ago, inspired in me the feeling that beauty is woven into the fabric of life.

A psychologist named Adolf Zeising believed that nature aims at beauty. In his view, a mathematical pattern known as the Golden Ratio repeatedly crops up the natural world. For example, the Golden Ratio can be discerned in seashells, plants, and other natural as well as manmade forms. We can think of the Golden Ratio as a motif that surfaces again and again in nature and also in the products of human culture, but in a variety of guises.

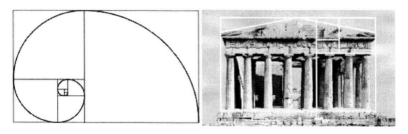

The Golden Ratio reflected in the architecture of the Greek Parthenon

The symmetry in nature suggests that there is a subtle order woven into the fabric of existence.

I like to think of beauty as health food for the soul. Beauty can take many forms. A church cathedral, a musical symphony, a glorious sunset, a meadow of flowers, or the smile of a loved one can fill my heart with a sense of gratitude for life's bounties. Indeed, there is something about beauty that seems to soothe my soul and align my spirit to the goodness in life.

The symmetrical swirl of a seashell, the simple elegance of an architectural work such as the Greek Parthenon, and the intricate formation of seeds at the center of a sunflower might at first glance appear to share little in common. However, each of these exhibits a symmetry, which we find pleasing and even beautiful.

Life is continually unfolding new forms of beauty. No sunrise, speckle-colored butterfly, or smile is ever quite the same as the ones that have come before. Each is unique and never-quite repeatable. But each individual example of beauty is a reflection of something deeper; namely, the principle of Beauty.

The idea that nature aims at beauty is a pretty remarkable thought. It suggests that there is an intrinsic order and a subtle intelligence woven into the fabric of life. Beauty kindles the imagination and inspires wonder. Beauty can even make us feel that we are in the presence of the divine. The philosopher Plato believed that contemplating beautiful things made the soul more beautiful. No doubt, experiencing beauty can help us to flourish.

Does nature really aim at beauty? There does appear to be much chaos, disorder, and ugliness in the world too. But perhaps chaos is just the backdrop, which is necessary for beauty and order to have their full import and meaning. Life would not have the meaning it has were it not for death. And perhaps love would not be as precious and sacred as it is without the possibility of loss.

There is a beauty in life that arises from the play of opposites. Beauty is often fragile, perishable, and fleeting. Beauty is all the more precious because of this. Individual instances of beauty spring into existence all the time . . . and they vanish all the time too. Individual instances of beauty are destined to perish, but the principle of beauty inspires wonder and love eternally.

Pay It Forward

"Sail beyond the horizon; fly higher than you ever thought possible; magnify your existence by helping others; be kind to people and animals of all shapes and sizes; be true to what you value most; shine your light on the world; and be the person you were born to be."

-- Blake Beattie

I like think of the world like a treasure chest. There are an abundance of gems and diamonds in the rough all around us. Some people uncover these treasures on a daily basis, others have to dig a little deeper to find them, and still others will never find or appreciate the riches that surround them.

For me, the spirit of generosity is one of the keys to unlocking the world's treasures. My parents believed that charity begins at home. Home is where it all starts. It is within our families that we first learn to empathize with others. A compassionate and understanding personality is the foundation upon which healthy communities depend. After all, a compassionate person naturally seeks to reach out to others to share the blessings they have received.

Pay it forward is a phrase that means being the recipient of a good deed, and in turn doing something good for someone else. I remember as a child and for most of my life, my parent's always reminded and encouraged my siblings and me to do good things for others. The maxim they taught us was simple: do unto to others as you would have them do to you. I remember my mom saying, "It may be just a very small act of kindness, but it can mean so much to someone else." It's a lesson I've taken to heart and in my experience doing good for others often makes you feel better about yourself. Albert Einstein put it well when he said, "A life lived for others is the only life worth living."

Years ago, when I was a child in grade school, I remember there were a few students attending our school from a local orphanage. In particular, I remember one boy was in need of a rain coat. I went home and asked my mother if we had a coat to spare for him. Sure enough, my mom found a suitable rain coat in the closet for him. I still remember the warm glow I felt when I brought that coat to school for him and saw the smile of gratitude on his face. From this and similar experiences I realized how enjoyable it can be to help others.

My father had great faith in the power of generosity. He had received many blessings in life, but he always displayed a keen desire to share his good fortune with deserving others. He also encouraged others to think and act charitably. For example, one Christmas my father asked his employees, if in lieu of their usual Christmas party, would it be agreeable to use the funds to buy gifts for the less fortunate. This probably was not an easy thing for my father's employees to give up, but they all agreed.

Unbeknownst to all, my father had already made a gift of his own. This collective act of charity helped make it a festive Christmas for some boys and girls at a local orphanage. My dad never made a fuss or display of his generosity. But I knew he took great pleasure in seeing the difference a donation could make in the lives of the needy. My dad never used the phrase "pay it forward," but that's just the kind of guy he was. Years later, I was deeply touched when so many of my father's employees recounted stories of my father's generosity at his funeral.

One night, I was visiting with my good friend, Mary, as we sat over a cup of coffee and chatted. Mary asked me about the charity walk I would be attending over the weekend for the Make-a-Wish Foundation. I knew Mary had other commitments and couldn't make the walk. She was also between jobs at the time, but without hesitation she said, "I want to write a check. I want to donate . . . . you know, pay it forward."

One of my most memorable pay it forward experiences happened while visiting Ireland. My boyfriend and I had hiked a couple of miles from the B & B where we were staying to the coastline for a day of sightseeing and a concert by Van Morrison in the evening. The day had been sunny and warm, but by the time the concert ended it was quite chilly. Finding a taxi proved surprisingly difficult, but thankfully a local couple overheard our plight and offered to share their taxi with us. Indeed, when they heard we were from the States they even insisted on picking up our share of the fare even though our destination was well out of their way. Their generosity is something we will always remember and my boyfriend and I both decided the best way to thank them was to pay it forward with a small donation to St. Jude Children's Hospital.

Hurricane Sandy devastated much of the north east. The Jersey Shore was hit quite hard and many homes were destroyed and people displaced. A good friend of mine, Karen, has a house at the shore. Karen's fiftieth birthday was approaching and her family asked how she would like to celebrate her birthday. Karen replied that she would like to have a barbeque at her place for all the neighbors who were displaced. Karen insisted that no one besides her family was to know it was her birthday. Knowing Karen, just seeing the smiles and appreciation from her neighbors was a birthday wish come true. It was also a great pay it forward moment.

The value of caring and sharing is first learned in the home. Today's world is filled with much hustle and bustle. Often, it seems difficult for today's parents to find quality time with their children. However, it is so important for young people to receive encouragement and empathy from their parents. Seeing young people exhibit concern and charity for others is inspiring. Recently, I had a heartwarming experience as I read a handmade sign at a lemonade stand that my grand niece and grand nephew had set up. I had expected the sign to be about the price of the lemonade, but instead it was all about how the proceeds of their sale would go to benefit Gilda's Club, a non-profit organization dedicated to helping people living with cancer, their families and friends. If more children learned the importance of a pay it forward attitude, then the world would be a brighter place.

Pay it forward is a simple idea that each of us can do to make the world a better place. Paying it forward may not be able to solve all the world's problems, but small acts of kindness have a way of reinforcing each other and adding up. Paying it forward doesn't require great wealth, just a caring heart. Just helping one person can make a difference. A kind act or thoughtful gesture may only take a moment, but the significance may last a lifetime. Good deeds can be contagious. When enough people engage in small acts of kindness it creates a virtuous cycle that benefits everyone. Together, we can change the world one step at a time with each small act of kindness.

The Myth of Orpheus and Eurydice

"Look not at the days gone by with a forlorn heart. They were simply the dots we can now connect with our present, to help us draw the outline of a beautiful tomorrow."

-- Dodinsky

"Bring the past only if you are going to build from it."

-- Doménico Cieri Estrada

Walking Out of Darkness is a title that can refer to a number of different journeys. It can refer to the path we take towards a better psychological state following the loss of a loved one. It can also refer to the journey we take in recovering from depression. And it can also pertain to the course we chart in overcoming disabilities or serious obstacles in our life.

Every individual is unique. There is no roadmap for recovery which will be valid for everyone in every circumstance. Nevertheless, one of the central messages in this book is this: if recovery is your goal, then focusing on the here and now is better than dwelling on the past.

The story of Orpheus and Eurydice is a myth that illustrates the wisdom of not allowing what is behind us to distract us from moving forward. In Ovid's tale, Orpheus is a musician with a divine gift to charm all living things with his sublimely beautiful music. Tragically, Orpheus' lover, Eurydice, is killed by a serpent's bite while she was out walking in the tall grass just before her wedding to Orpheus. Orpheus is so overcome with grief that he ventures deep into the underworld in a seemingly futile quest to convince Hades, lord of the underworld, to restore Eurydice to life.

For an eternity, Hades remained unmoved by the pleas of mortals. On this one occasion, however, Hades was so shaken by the soul-stirring music of Orpheus that he agreed to allow Orpheus to see Eurydice and take her from the underworld, but on a few conditions: Eurydice must travel behind Orpheus on their journey back to the world of the living and Orpheus must not look backwards until both have crossed the threshold into the land of the living. If Orpheus looks back, then Hades will reclaim Eurydice.

Orpheus agrees, but the further he ascends towards the earth the fainter his beloved Eurydice's footsteps seem to be. His anxiety, fed by Eurydice's increasingly soft footsteps, proves too much to bear; he turns just a moment too soon and Eurydice vanishes from his sight, this time forever.

The myth of Orpheus and Eurydice highlights the pitfalls of dwelling too much on the past. Orpheus would have conquered death had he kept his focus forward. Instead, he turned his gaze backwards, into the past, just as he was about to enter the world of the living.

Similarly, an excessive preoccupation with the past can keep us from moving forward and living life fully. In particular, allowing past losses, regrets, disappointments, and unresolved grievances to cast shadows on the present hinders our ability to enjoy the only time any of us are guaranteed, the here and now.

Scheherazade's Triumph Over Death

We are mortal creatures. Each of us knows that we will draw our last breath at some point in the future. Most of us, who are not yet old, imagine that our destiny is on the distant horizon. However, the prospect that we could die tomorrow is something that each of us recognizes as a possibility.

The story of Scheherazade, from the *The Arabian Nights*, illustrates this aspect of the human predicament. Scheherazade is a woman who faces a sentence of death at the hands of a ruthless, capricious, and misogynistic king. Sometime before, the king had been betrayed by his lover. To exact his revenge against womanhood he takes a concubine each night to his bed, but he then executes her the very next morning after he has satisfied his lust.

Recognizing what fate has in store for her, Scheherazade devises a plan to save her life; each night she will spin a fantastic tale that so enraptures the king that he will feel compelled to learn how it ends. The king is enchanted by Scheherazade's stories, but each night he falls asleep before his captive mistress can finish her tale. Night after night this pattern repeats itself with the king increasingly absorbed by the narrative web spun by Scheherazade. Ultimately, Scheherazade manages to weave in a tale about a pitiless ruler who pardons a woman he has condemned to death because she teaches him to love again. The king, smitten by Scheherazade and her fables, recognizes that his heart has been transformed. Scheherazade finds redemption, the two are married, and she bears him three heirs. Scheherazade had spun her stories out of her own substance. Her love transformed the heart of a seemingly merciless tyrant and brought her a triumph over death.

Like Scheherazade, we humans are natural storytellers. We seem to be creatures with an instinct for beauty, meaning, and transcendence. Like plants, which turn their petals to the sun, we humans seek and our propelled by the desire for love. Indeed, the quest for love is invariably the basis for so many enduring works of art, literature, and music.

When we imbue our stories (and other creative endeavors) with love, then we create narratives and works that have the capacity to inspire and transform the hearts of others. The story I have shared with you was borne out of great loss, but I believe at least some of the beauty, goodness, and light my departed loved ones shared with me has been woven into this book. I sincerely hope that you will have found something within these pages that will help you on your journey walking out of darkness.

Conclusion: Spreading Your Wings

Not every day is good, but there is good in every day.

-- Alice Morse Earle

The butterfly is a symbol of hope and transcendence.

As we come to the close of this book, we, the authors, hope you continue with the next chapter of your life discovering and appreciating all the beauty that surrounds you. Whether confronting the death of a loved one, family issues, work pressures, financial burdens, or simply the daily grind, remember there is beauty, goodness, and love in the world. If these qualities seem hard to find, then it is up to each and every one of us to try and create them. Keep in mind, progress is made by individuals who make the decision to light a candle rather than curse the darkness.

The path out of darkness is not always easy to tread. Sometimes, it can seem like we are caterpillars inching our way towards some impossibly remote destination. But like the homely caterpillar, each of us contains within ourselves the power of transcending our circumstances. Just as the earth-bound caterpillar sheds its cocoon and is reborn as a winged butterfly, we, too, can rise above our circumstances and emerge freer and more fully alive than ever before.

The transformation of a caterpillar into a butterfly is one of nature's most remarkable processes. It is a process that seems to symbolize life's capacity for transcendence. Sometimes, we must go beyond ourselves, so that we may find a great wind and spread our wings.

A Note from the Authors

Walking Out of Darkness is a book that reflects two perspectives, which the authors have attempted to weave into a seamless whole. The experiences we relate are real, but the point of view we arrive at is the byproduct of two souls searching for the truth through dialogue. Hopefully, this makes for a book that is greater than the sum of its parts.

The book is largely told from the perspective of Bridget Carley. The experiences she relates are hers, but her co-author, Scott O'Reilly, has made important contributions to how this story is told. Generally speaking, our aim has been to make the personal universal. More specifically, as we discussed the experiences and ideas in this book we found that our perspectives tended to complement one another. As a result, the words in our book are something we arrived at jointly after many hours of thoughtful discussion.

We do not claim to be experts, but we do hope the thoughts and experiences in this book contain some hard-won wisdom. Most of all, we hope this book can be both a comfort and source of hope for our fellow travelers who may be facing loss and adversity. If you have any feedback on our book, or would like to share an inspiring story or a personal experience of your own, we would like to hear from you. Please contact us at: (Bridget) beaswax@optonline.net or (Scott) neuroscott@aol.com. Thank you for reading our book and may you always find some light to guide you on your journey.

Acknowledgements

Every book, like every life, has many people to thank for its existence. The authors of this book would like to gratefully acknowledge the help, feedback, encouragement, and support of the following friends and family. For reading early drafts and providing feedback we would especially like to thank Bob & Anne Waldron and Joe & Cheryl Carley. For sharing the inspiring story of their mom, Mary Grace, we would like to thank Eileen and Karen. For friendship, encouragement, listening, and psychological support we would like to thank Mary, Cathy, Anne, Clare, Kathi, Lisa, and Val & Tony. For her friendship and sharing her inspiring story of recovery we would like to thank Libby. For always being a beacon of light and spiritual support we would like to thank Sister Elizabeth and Sister Mary. For recollections about Bridget's mom & dad and Pat and Jim we would like to thank Carley Anne & George, Robert & Marianne, Kaitlin & Mike, Joseph III, Patrick, and Shannon. We would also like to thank Kieran & Marie O'Reilly, Shane O'Reilly, and Dennis & Fiona Leonard. We would also like to give thanks to Joseph, Mary, Pat and Jim. The love they shared during their lifetimes helped make this book possible.

About the Authors

Bridget Anne Carley earned her Bachelor's degree in Sociology from Merrimack College. She has worked in the social services as both a counselor and probation officer. For nearly twenty years, Bridget was the business manager at Wyckoff Ford in New Jersey. Today, she is an active participant in the bereavement community and a hospice volunteer. *Walking Out of Darkness* is her first book.

Scott David O'Reilly is an independent writer. He graduated from Fairfield University where he majored in psychology and philosophy. His articles have appeared in *The Humanist, Philosophy Now, The National Catholic Reporter,* and numerous other publications.